GB
NL
GERMANY
LUX.
FRANCE
SWITZER-LAND
ITALY
PROVENCE
SPAIN
Briancon
L'Olan 3564
Vallouise
PARC NATIONAL DES ECRINS
Abriès
Arvieux
Queyras
Chauffayer
Durance
Col dell'Angelo 2748
St-Véran
Monviso 3841
Orcières
Guillestre
Casteldelfino
Embrun
Gap
Chorges
Barrage de Serre Poncon
Savines-le-Lac
Mey-ronnes
Acceglio
Cùneo
Mondovì
Le Lauzet-Ubaye
Col de Maddalena 1995
ITALIA (ITALY)
Barce-lonnette
Selonnet
Viàdio
Vernante
Barles
Terme di Valdieri
Colle di Tenda 1279
Argentera 3297
steron
Colmars
Entraunes
Tende
ALPES MARITIMES
St-Martin-Vesubie
Château-Arnoux
Digne
Verdon
Saorge
ALPES DE PROVENCE
St-André-les-Alpes
Barrême
Les Scaffarels
Paget-Théniers
San Remo
Brillane
Castellane
Ste-Marie
Gréolières
MONACO
Venti-miglia
Menton
Monte Carlo
Lac de St-Croix
Aiguines
Trigance
Vence
Nice
Beaulieu
Villefranche
Grand Canyon du Verdon
Grasse
VAR
Aups
Antibes
Lac de St-Cassien
Cannes
CÔTE D'AZUR
Barjols
Salernes
Draguignan
Lorgues
Fréjus
St-Raphael
CORNICHE DE L'ESTEREL
Brignoles
Ste-Maxime
St-Tropez
La Môle
Cuers
Toulon
Hyères
La-Londe-les-Maures
Le Lavandou
CORNICHE MAURES
ix-Fours-es-Plages
La Tour-Fondue
I. DU LEVANT
ILES D'HYERES
Mediterranean Sea
I. DE PORQUEROLLES
I. DE PORT-CROS

France
100 miles / 160 km
Dundee
Glasgow
Firth of Forth
Edinburgh
North Channel
Belfast
Newcastle upon Tyne
Carlisle
Sunderland
Middlesbrough
UNITED
KINGDOM
ISLE OF MAN
Irish Sea
York
Kingston upon Hull
Leeds
Manchester
Holyhead
Liverpool
Sheffield
Stoke-on-Trent
Derby
Nottingham
Wolverhampton
Leicester
Norwich
Birmingham
Coventry
Cambridge
Wales
Fishguard
Ipswich
Oxford
Swansea
Cardiff
London
Bristol Channel
Bristol
Reading
Southampton
Portsmouth
Bournemouth
Brighton
ISLE OF WIGHT
Plymouth
Dover
Oostende
Calais
English Channel
North Sea
Randers
Arhus
DENMARK
Esbjerg
Odense
FYN
Lolland
NORTH FRISIAN ISLANDS
Flensburg
Kiel
Lübeck
Hamburg
EAST FRISIAN ISLANDS
Groningen
Bremen
Elbe
NETHERLANDS
Jsselmeer
Hannover
Amsterdam
Den Haag
Utrecht
Bielefeld
Münster
Essen
Dortmund
Rotterdam
Duisburg
Bochum
Kassel
Düsseldorf
Erfurt
Antwerpen
Bruxelles
Wuppertal
Köln
Liège
Bonn
GERMANY
Lille
BELGIUM
Koblenz
Wiesbaden
Main
Frankfurt
Mainz
LUXEMBOURG
Amiens
Saint Quentin
Luxembourg
Rhein
Mannheim
Cherbourg
Le Havre
Rouen
GUERNSEY
JERSEY
Seine
Reims
Meuse
Metz
Saarbrücken
Karlsruhe
Stuttgart
Paris
Versailles
Brest
Saint Malo
Nancy
Strasbourg
Ulm
Donau
Rennes
Troyes
Lorient
Sens
Auxerre
Orléans
Le Mans
Mulhouse
Bodensee
BELLE ÎLE
Angers
Tours
Loire
Avallon
Nantes
Basel
Zürich
Dijon
Autun
Besançon
Bern
SWITZERLAND
FRANCE
Beaune
Lausanne
Cluny
Châteauroux
Allier
Mâcon
Genfer See
Loire
Genève
ÎLE DE RÉ
La Rochelle
Belleville
Bergamo
Atlantic
ÎLE D'OLÉRON
Clermont-Ferrand
Mont Blanc
4807
Como
Lyon
Limoges
Saint Étienne
Grenoble
Milano
Torino
Po
Ocean
Brive
Valence
ITALY
Bordeaux
Dordogne
Rhône
Genova
Orange
Bay of Biscay
La Spezia
Garonne
PROVENCE
San Remo
Nîmes
Avignon
Nice
Bayonne
Montpellier
MONACO
Ligurian Sea
Toulouse
Cannes
Santander
Béziers
Bilbao
Pau
Marseille
Toulon
CAP CORSE
San Sebastian
PYRENEES
Perpignan
Vitoria
Pamplona
Bastia
CORSICA
ANDORRA
3404
Pico de Aneto
Burgos
Logroño
Ebro
Gerona
Ajaccio
Valladolid
Mediterranean Sea
Duero
Strait of Bonifacio
Zaragosa
Olbia
Barcelona
Sassari
SPAIN
Tarragona
SARDINIA

Provence

Written and Presented by **Mark Fincham**

Mark Fincham

INSIGHT POCKET GUIDES

Insight Pocket Guide:
PROVENCE

Directed by
Hans Höfer

Managing Editor
Andrew Eames

Photography by
Gil Galvin and George Taylor

Design Concept by
V. Barl

Design by
Carlotta Junger

© 1993 APA Publications (HK) Ltd

All Rights Reserved

Printed in Singapore by
Höfer Press (Pte) Ltd
Fax: 65-8616438

Distributed in the United States by
Houghton Mifflin Company
2 Park Street
Boston, Massachusetts 02108
ISSN: 0-395-66903-0

Distributed in Canada by
Thomas Allen & Son
390 Steelcase Road East
Markham, Ontario L3R 1G2
ISSN: 0-395-66903-0

Distributed in the UK & Ireland by
GeoCenter International UK Ltd
The Viables Center, Harrow Way
Basingstoke, Hampshire RG22 4BJ
ISBN: 9-62421-567-7

Worldwide distribution enquiries:
Höfer Communications Pte Ltd
38 Joo Koon Road
Singapore 2262
ISBN: 9-62421-567-7

NO part of this book may be reproduced, stored in a retrieval system or transmitted in any form or means electronic, mechanical, photocopying, recording or otherwise, without prior written permission of Apa Publications. Brief text quotations with use of photographs are exempted for book review purposes only.
As every effort is made to provide accurate information in this publication, we would appreciate it if readers would call our attention to any errors that may occur by communicating with Apa Villa, 81 The Cut, London SE1 8LL. Tel: 71-620-0008, Fax: 71-620-1074.
Information has been obtained from sources believed to be reliable, but its accuracy and completeness, and the opinions based thereon, are not guaranteed.

Bienvenue!

Welcome! I first came to Provence in the summer of 1982 and remember long hot days of idleness and pleasure. At the time I did not think I had been especially smitten, but when summer came round again I found myself thinking only of Provence. Then I found myself arriving for the *réveillon,* the celebration of the New Year when the skies are blown clear by the mistral. Soon I was coming for Easter and then for the *vendange* (grape harvest). Finally I bowed to the inevitable and came to stay, following a trend that began 2,000 years ago when retiring Roman senators built their villas in what we now know as Aix-en-Provence.

In *Insight Pocket Guide: Provence* I have designed a series of itineraries to help you extract the essential magic of Provence. I begin at the foot of the Mt-Ventoux, known as the *géant* (giant) of Provence, and take you on a tour around the Dentelles de Montmirail. I then turn south to Avignon, ancient Rhône staging post and once home to the popes, from where it is a short hop to Arles, a fascinating and culturally diverse town. From here I move on to Aix-en-Provence, Italianate and sophisticated. From Aix I head for the fishing port of Cassis, the unique Ile de Porquerolles and incomparable St-Tropez, to my mind the highlights of this sublime Mediterranean coast. Afterwards I turn inland to my own patch of Provence, the tranquil Var, and then return to our starting point with a roller-coaster ride through the stone villages of the Luberon. Itineraries include restaurant recommendations — a subject close to my heart — and point you to the *caves* of Provence's best vintners. I hope that as you enjoy a glass or two, you will remember me.

Welcome! Bienvenue! — Mark Fincham

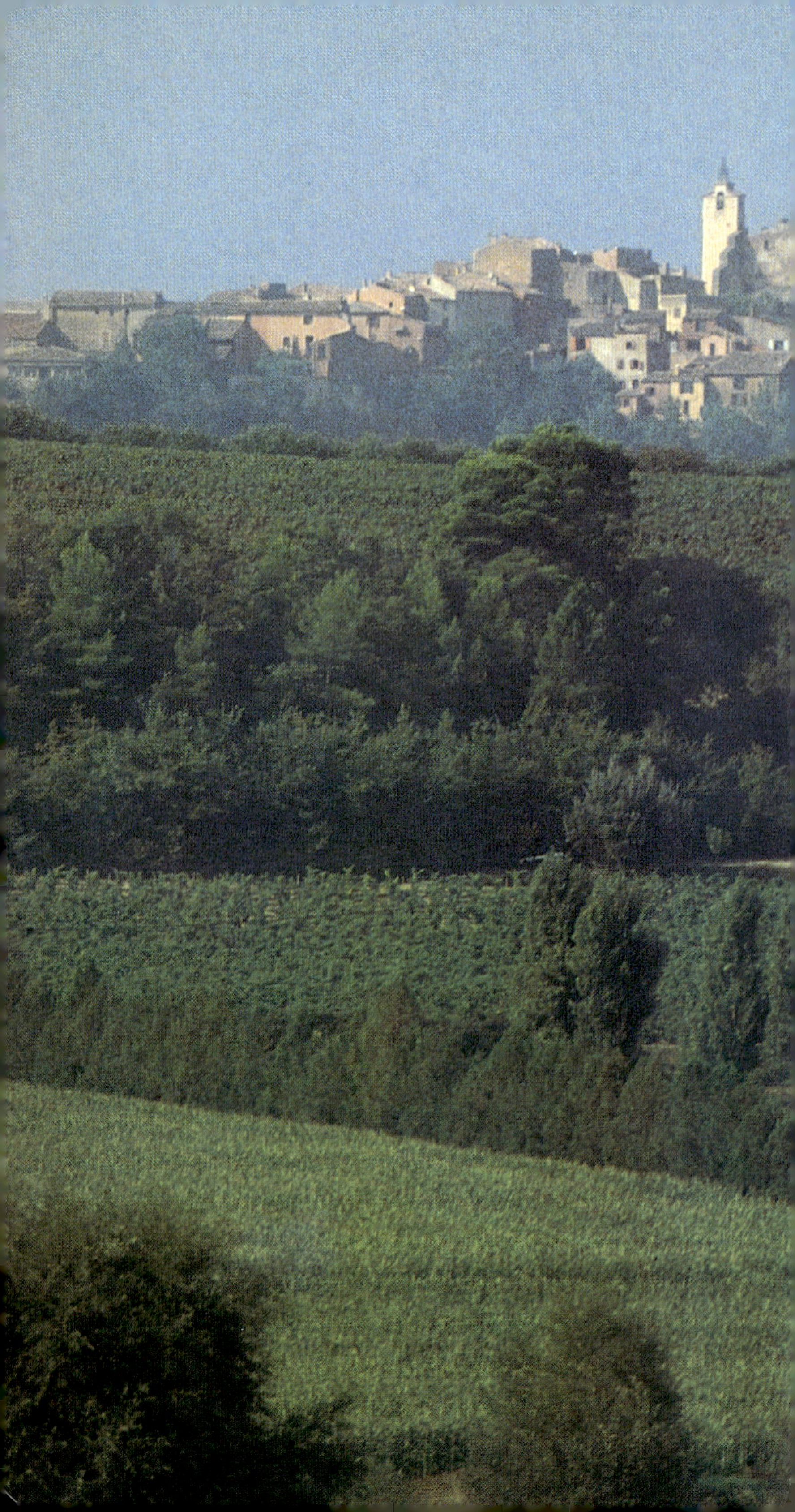

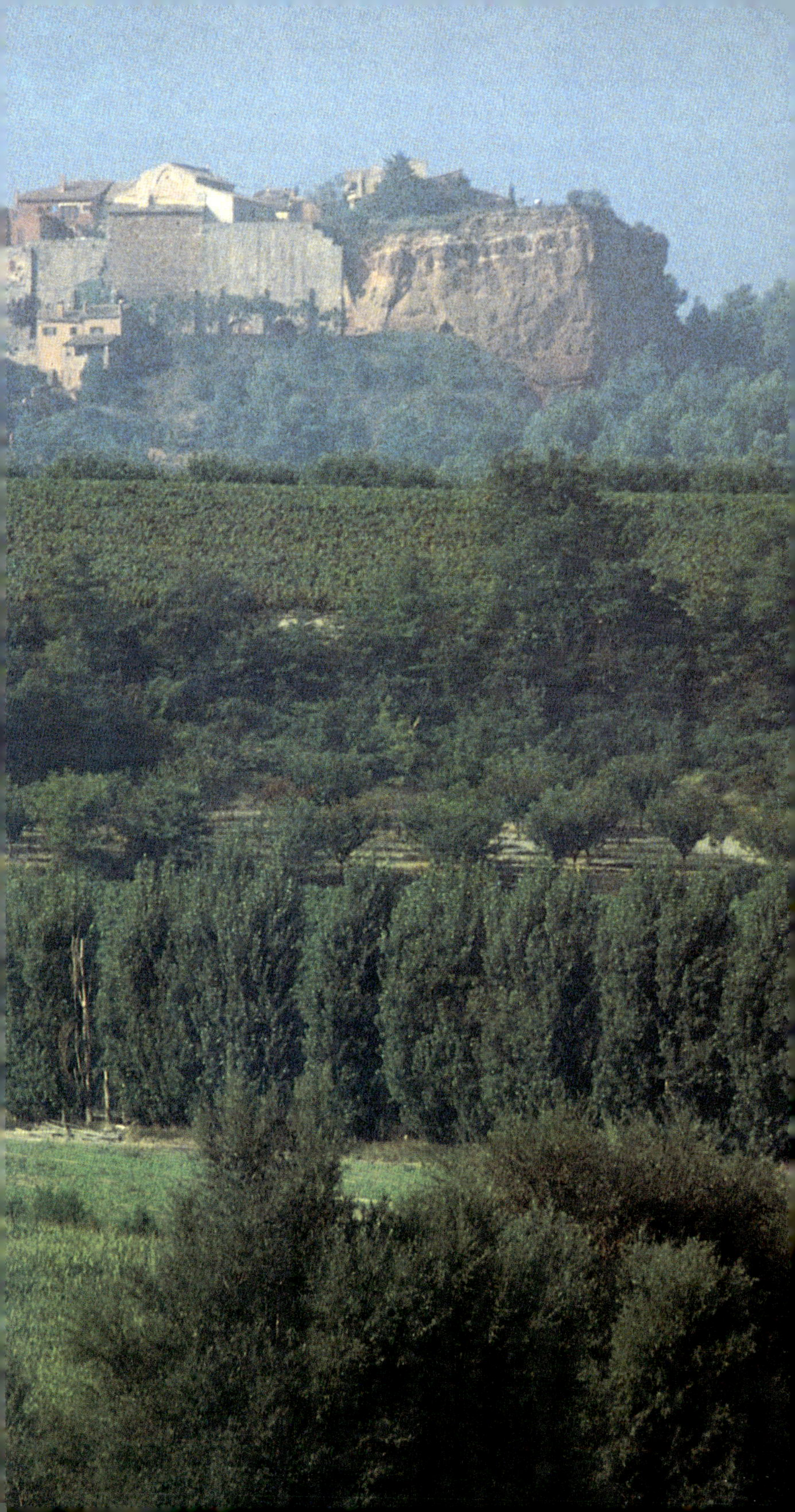

Contents

Welcome..5
History and Culture..........................12
   The Greeks.......................................12
   The Romans.....................................13
   The Christians.................................14
   A New Breed of Visitor...................16
   The Provençals................................17
   Historical Highlights.......................19

Day Itineraries
The Vaucluse
   1. Picturesque Provence....................**23**
   2. Option: Mt-Ventoux........................**28**
Avignon
   3. Papal City and Vineyard Country........**30**
Arles
   4. Roman Morning, Rural Afternoon........**36**
   5. Option: The Camargue..................**41**
Aix-en-Provence
   6. From the Renaissance to Cézanne......**42**
   7. Option: Marseille........................**47**
Along the Coast
   8. Cassis......................................**49**
   9. Ile de Porquerolles.....................**51**
   10. St-Tropez................................**52**
The Var
   11. A Circuit in the Hills....................**55**
   12. Option: A Lake and a Canyon..........**59**
The Luberon
   13. Le Pays d'Apt............................**60**

Shopping...**66**
Eating Out...**70**
Calendar of Special Events.............**78**

Practical Information
Getting There....................................**80**
   By Air, By Rail, By Car......................**80**
   Driving, Speed Limits.......................**81**

Preceding pages: the village of Roussillon in the Luberon

Travel Essentials **82**
  Visas and Passports, When to Visit,
  Clothing, Electricity................................**82**
  Time..**83**
Money Matters **83**
  Banks, Currency, Credit Cards,
  Cash Machines, Tipping **83**
Holidays and Hours..................................**83**
  Business Hours, Public Holidays............**83**
Accommodation **84**
  Hotels **84**
Nightlife..**88**
Health & Emergencies **89**
  Police and Crime **89**
  Fires..**90**
Post & Communications **90**
  Post, Telephone, Media........................**90**
Information & Maps..............................**90**
Language **91**
Useful Addresses **91**
Further Reading......................................**91**
Index **92**

Maps
Provence **IFC–1**
France **2**
The Vaucluse **26**
Avignon **31**
Vineyard Country **32**
Arles **37**
Les Alpilles and The Camargue..................**38**
Aix-en-Provence **43**
Cézanne Country **45**
The Provençal Coast **48**
St-Tropez **53**
The Var **56**
The Luberon..**61**

*Following pages:
the harbour at Cassis*

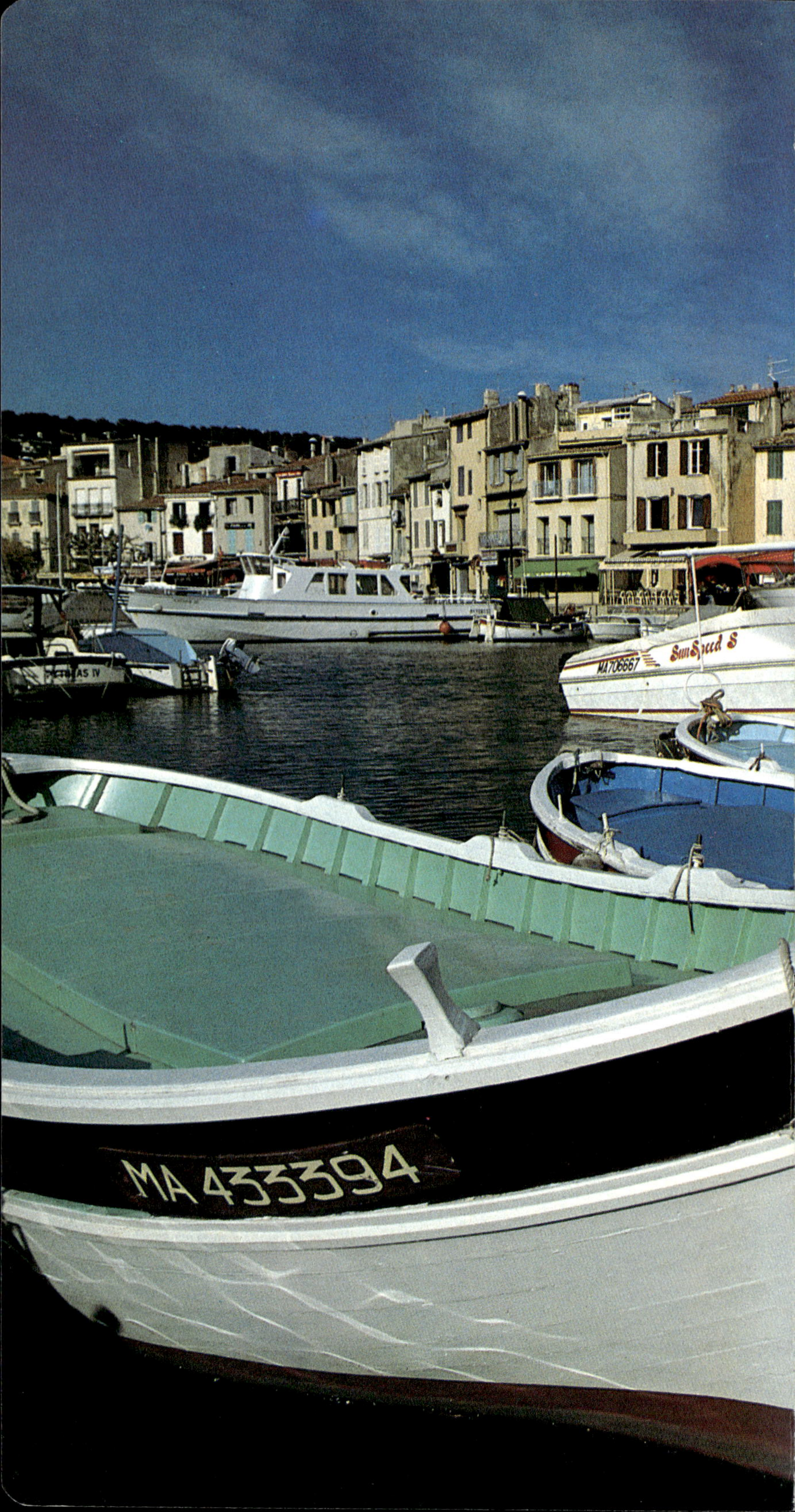
MA 433394
MA706667

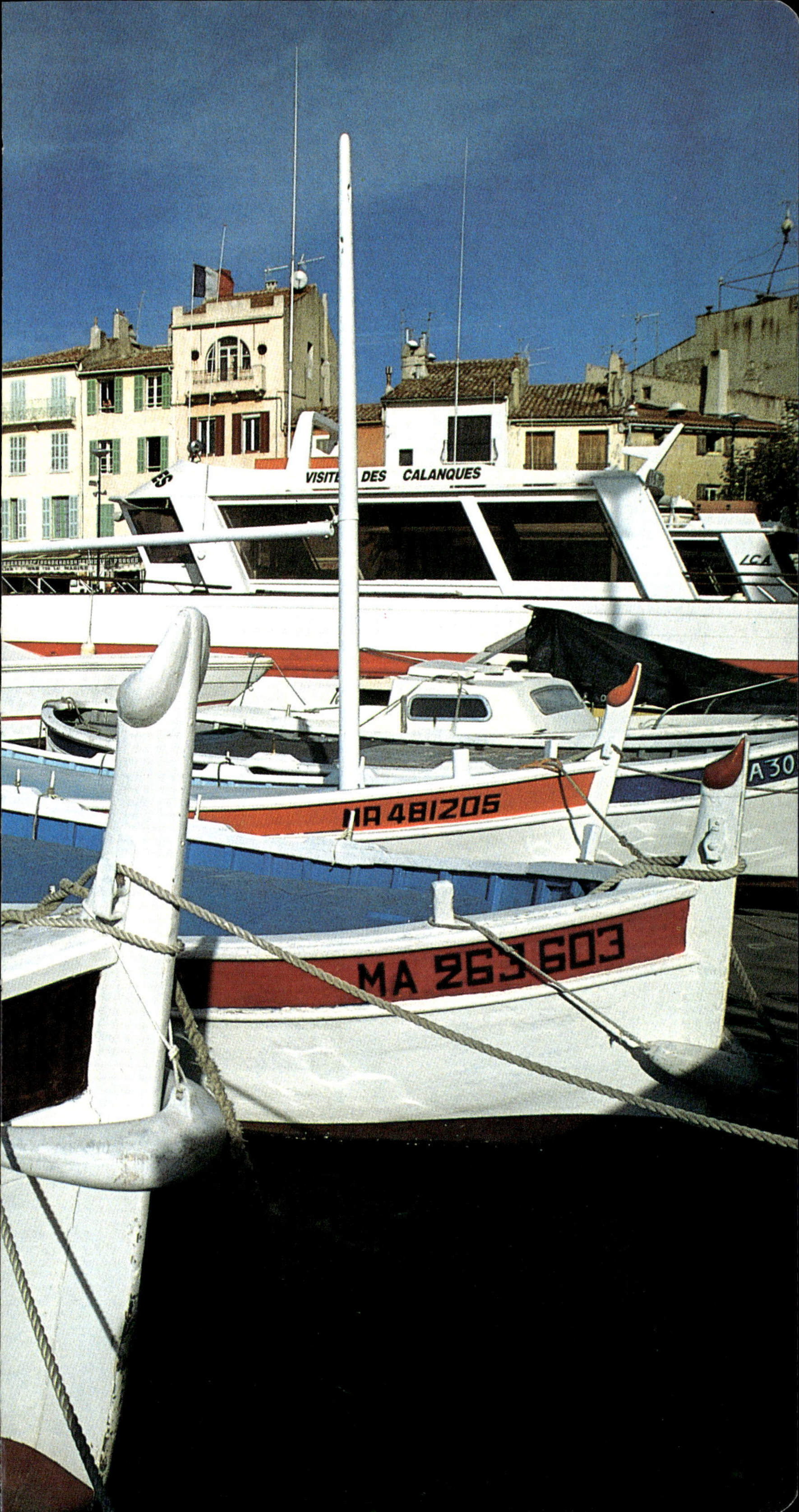
VISITE DES CALANQUES
MA 481205
MA 263 603

HISTORY

In his book on Provence, Ford Madox Ford described the region as 'a highway along which travelled continuously the stream of the arts, of thought, of the traditions of life'. The process he so aptly describes has created what I would identify as the supreme type of the Mediterranean culture. The presiding genius is, of course, that great *donné*, the sun. Its characteristic features are the products of the olive and grape, the universal cafés, the *cours* and *boulevards* where people meet and talk, the customary evening promenade, the *apéritif* and the game of *boules*, the love of running water expressed in the ubiquitous fountains, the many social and cultural manifestations such as village fêtes, markets, concerts and theatre and, in winter, the devotion to the *chasse*. In this brief history I hope to give at least some idea of how this all came about.

The Greeks first introduced the vine

The Greeks

The Greeks who came to Provence in 600BC are attributed with introducing the techniques for cultivating vines. Today vineyards cover 40,000 hectares (155 sq. miles) of land, or nearly half the

Culture

area with agricultural usage. They are the characteristic of the Provençal countryside, and their wines are found on every table. The other gift of the Greeks was the olive tree. Though less extensive than the vine, it has nevertheless contributed to another of the definitive characteristics of Provençal culture – a cuisine based on olive oil (as opposed to butter).

The overriding dominance of the vine in the Provençal countryside has been steadily reduced over the last 50 years as irrigation schemes have enabled intensive cultivation of fruits and vegetables less suited to dry conditions. These schemes include the taming of the Durance and Verdon rivers by building dams at Serre-Ponçon and Saint-Croix, and the creation of Le Canal de Provence which feeds a 3,000-km (1,850-mile) system of irrigation canals. The intensive cultivation of peaches, apples and sunflowers which are such a distinctive feature in the Vaucluse and Bouches-de-Rhône regions was unknown 25 years ago. Today Provence accounts for 35 percent of national production of vegetables and 25 percent of fruits.

The Romans

In 122BC the Romans founded their first settlement in Provence after a victory over the indigenous tribes, variously described as Franks or Gauls. The site, named Aquae Sextiae, would eventually become Aix-en-Provence. This was the beginning of Roman rule in Provence and it lasted until the fall of the Roman Empire in AD476. Curiously, the Romans had originally come

Roman ruins at St Remy

to Provence to help their traditional allies, the Greeks, whose trading ambitions were hindered by the Gauls. However, they increasingly began to see Provence as a stepping-stone between Italy and Spain, the spoil of their victory over the Carthaginians. They also liked what they found and named it *Provincia* – the Roman province. In 103BC the Roman general Marius consolidated Rome's hold on the area by defeating a huge army of Teutons from northern Europe. The name Marius has lived on in the common memory and until recently was a common boy's name in Provence.

Unlike the Greeks who came to Provence to trade, the Romans were true imperialists. The whole cultural apparatus of Rome was imposed on the new province. Towns were built according to the Roman urban plan and each one had its own individual forum, arena, theatre, public baths and fountains, and three great roads were constructed to link them – the Aurelian Way, the Agrippan Way and the Domitian Way.

Vestiges of this titanic building programme can be seen all over Provence, in small bridges and ruins and often in antique remains incorporated into the walls of contemporary buildings, as in the Nord-Pinus Hotel in Arles. Then there are the mighty public buildings of Frejus, Arles, Nîmes, Orange and Vaison. This heritage has profoundly influenced the shape of present-day Provence. The central *cours* or *place* and the fountain of every town and village are derived from the Roman forum. In Aix-en-Provence these fountains are the Roman signature on a town that at first sight bears little imprint of its Roman history, for they are animated by the thermal springs, the *aquae* after which Sextius named this site.

The great Roman arenas of Frejus, Arles, Nîmes and Orange are a graphic illustration of the way in which Provence has absorbed and adapted its past. One moment they are mute witnesses to Provençal history, the next a vital part of contemporary cultural life, as venues for concerts and bullfights. At the moment when the matador is lining up for the kill and the crowd quietens in anticipation it is impossible to imagine that the arena ever existed for any other purpose.

The Christians

Christianity, no less than the Greeks or the Romans, left its imprint on the complicated grid of Provençal history. From the legendary conversion of Provence to Christianity in the 1st

Early representations of Christ

Baronial coat of arms

century, after the miraculous landing of the boat from Judea – the so-called Boat of Bethany – bearing amongst others, Lazarus, Mary Magdalene and Martha, religion has exerted a strong influence.

Monasticism took an early hold and in the 12th century the Cistercians built the great Romanesque abbeys of Sénanque, Silvacane and Thoronet. Perhaps not surprisingly the heavy, simple forms of the Romanesque – with their reminder of classical shapes – struck a chord in Provence, unleashing an intense period of building activity. Romanesque churches from this period are a distinctive feature of many Provençal villages.

Provence was also a destination for pilgrims who came to the superb Gothic basilica of St Maximin, which stands on the spot where, according to legend, Mary Magdalene was buried. The papacy came to Avignon in the 14th century putting Provence, for a short while, at the centre of the Christian world. Though the popes returned to Rome in 1377, they retained control of an area known as the *Comtat Venaissin* (today the department of the Vaucluse) and their influence and the magnificent legacy of their building continued to inform the life of this area, notably in the Religious Wars of the 16th century when many Protestant villages in the Luberon were destroyed.

Though religious observance has declined, the Christian history of Provence informs the *fêtes* that are part of the cultural life of every village. Some are clearly part of the Christian tradition, such as the *fêtes* of the Nativity on Christmas Eve, when the Nativity is enacted by members of the village (one of the best known of these is in the village of Seguret in the Vaucluse). This is itself an extension of the popular Provençal custom of decorating a crib with *santons* – clay figures representing the cast of the Nativity. Collections of these figures are found in all the museums devoted to popular culture and are considered typically Provençal. In fact, like so many things, this practice was imported from Italy in

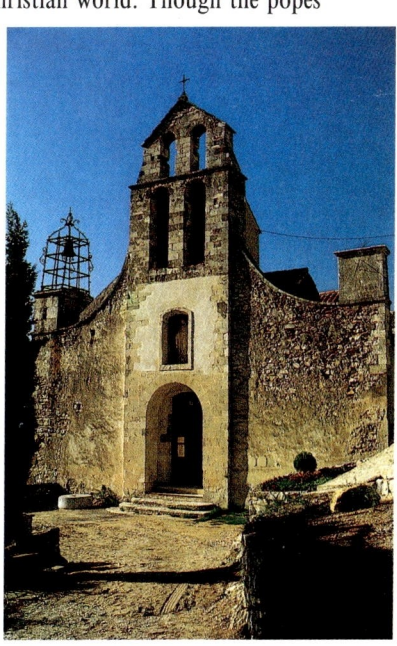

The Romanesque church at Gigondas

'Houses in Provence' by Cézanne, who was born in Aix-en-Provence

the 16th century and rapidly incorporated into Provençal culture.

In many cases the Christian foundations of a *fête* have been forgotten or overlayed with a new meaning and the *fête* has become a popular celebration. One such is the rowdy *Bravade* of 16 May in St-Tropez celebrating the naming of the town after the Roman martyr Torpes (Tropez), who was decapitated after converting to Christianity and washed up in the one-time fishing port which bears his name. More famous is the *Fête et pélerinage* to Les-Saintes-Maries-de-la-Mer. The 700-year-old annual pilgrimage to the town where the Boat of Bethany landed is now famous as a two-day festival of the gypsies. Their patron saint is Sarah, the slave of the Marys (Magdalene, Salomé and Jacobé) who arrived in the boat.

A New Breed of Visitor

In 1763 the English writer Tobias Smollett travelled to the South of France in search of a climate that might restore his health. He did not find this an agreeable experience but the published account of his travels brought the climate of the south, particularly the crisp, dry winters, to the attention of a larger public. He wrote, 'There is less rain and wind at Nice than in any other part of the world that I know... [the] air being dry, pure, heavy, and elastic, must be agreeable to the constitution of those who labour under disorders, arising from weak nerves, obstructed perspiration... a viscidity of lymph, and a languid circulation.' Since this described a wide variety of disorders he was soon followed by coach-loads of invalids, and also by the English aristocracy, who took to wintering on the Riviera to escape the damp and cold of England.

For these first tourists the season lasted only from November to March. The summer was considered hot and unhealthy until the 1920s, when a few daring Americans persuaded one hotel owner to remain open in the summer.

The French were generally less excited by the discovery of the South of France, though they established resorts in Hyères and St-Raphael. The introduction of the paid holiday in 1936 – two weeks statutory minimum – changed all that, and they too began flocking to the south, many of them in order to see the sea for the first time.

A parallel development was a migration of artists and writers to the South of France. The artists were attracted by the clarity of the Mediterranean light and the writers drawn by the cheap living conditions. The first artists whose work publicised the area and shaped people's perceptions of it were the painters Van Gogh, Cézanne and Paul Signac. A number of writers were also influential, among whom Colette, F Scott Fitzgerald, Somerset Maugham and Françoise Sagan all published books set in Provence. They contributed to a rising tide of publicity that created the image of a warm Mediterranean paradise and helped establish the reputation of Provence as the place for those interested in the arts.

All this publicity was as nothing compared to the tumult that was unleashed by one *artiste* at the end of the 1950s. Her name was Brigitte Bardot and the scenes of her making love and swimming naked at St-Tropez in the film *And God Created Woman*, brought St-Tropez and Provence to the notice of the world, and brought the world to St-Tropez and Provence. In 1988 the number of visitors to Provence had risen to 20 million, attracted by the myth fostered by Brigitte Bardot, the opportunities for leisure offered by a climate averaging 2,800 hours of sunshine per annum and the rich cultural environment. Today tourism is the primary economy of Provence.

Year-round sun brought tourism

The Provençals

What are the people like who preside over all this? Well, as we have seen, since antiquity Provence has been one of the great highways of Europe, witnessing the earliest displacements of man and where the Mediterranean races have been assimilated. In the Arles region, the influence of Spain can be seen in the people and the customs, most obviously in the bullfight; the last major influx were refugees from the Spanish Civil War. In the coastal region around Marseilles the people are still said to bear the imprint of their Greek heritage. In the Var and the area around Nice the influence of Italy can be

The Provençal language

seen. Nice was an Italian possession for centuries and received, along with the Var, a large influx of Italians at the end of the 19th century. Since 1950 the south of France has received many settlers from Algeria, Tunisia and Morocco. They have been accommodated less smoothly than the Mediterranean races but their influence is already apparent, witness the increasing popularity of *couscous*.

These influxes have made for an open society, where the foreigner is not an object of suspicion. Provençals are generally welcoming and they enjoy contact with other people, particularly if this leads to a large general discussion. Their philosophy is live and let live. Paradoxically, however, this does not always extend to their own countrymen.

This attitude can be traced deep in the history of Provence, a history of separation and independence from the rest of France. Politically it was not joined to the kingdom of France until 1481. Culturally its links were with the Mediterranean countries. French did not replace Provençal as the official language of Provence until 1539. The papal court in Avignon conducted its affairs in Latin and Provençal – known as the *langue d'oc*. As Provence came increasingly under the sway of the centralising and unifying power of the state in the 19th century, a movement arose called the *Félibrige*, whose essential aim was to assert and preserve its cultural independence, including the revival of interest in the *langue d'oc*.

One of the best reasons for visiting Provence

Historical Highlights

600BC Greek traders found the port of Marseille, bringing with them the olive tree and the vine to Provence.
122 Foundation of Aquae-Sextiae (Aix-en-Provence) by the Romans.
103 Marius defeats the Teutons.
58–51 Subjugation of Gaul by Julius Caesar. Romans impose imperial rule on their new province.
19 Building of the Pont du Gard, which still exists today.
12 Romans occupy the settlement at Vaison.
AD46 The Boat of Bethany lands at Les Saintes-Maries-de-la-Mer.
476 Fall of the Roman Empire.
500 Vaison is invaded by the Burgundians.
536 Provence comes under the rule of the Franks.
1032 Provence is annexed to the Holy Roman Empire.
1125 The flowering of Troubador poetry and the Courts of Love, exemplified in Les Baux.
1152 Consecration of the church of St-Trophime.
1160 Foundation of the abbey of Sénanque.
1309 Clement V, a Frenchman, is given the papal crown.
1316 Pope John XXII establishes the papacy in Avignon.
1388 The eastern part of Provence, known as the County of Nice, comes under the rule of the House of Savoy (Italy).
1409 University of Aix is founded.
1481 Provence is joined to the kingdom of France.
1539 French replaces Provençal, the *langue d'oc*, as the official language.
1545 Destruction of Protestant villages in the Luberon during the Wars of Religion.
1763 English writer Tobias Smollett travels through the South of France; his writing attracted the first tourists – even though it wasn't entirely complimentary.
1789 The French Revolution.
1790 Provence is divided into three *départements*: Basse-Alpes, Bouches-du-Rhône and Var.
1815 The end of the Napoleonic Wars, the English aristocracy begins to winter in the south of France.
1839 Cézanne is born in Aix-en-Provence.
1854 Founding of the *Félibrige*.
1855 Building of the Paris to Avignon railway.
1860 The County of Nice is returned to France.
1865 Nice is linked by rail to Marseille and the valley of the Rhône.
1869 Publication of Daudet's *Lettres de Mon Moulin*.
1887 The term Côte d'Azur is coined.
1888 Van Gogh settles in Arles.
1892 Paul Signac the pontillist painter settles in St-Tropez.
1923 Regulations for the production of wines in Châteauneuf-du-Pape are introduced.
1925 The writer Colette moves to St Tropez.
1936 Introduction of the paid holiday in France.
1941 Bandol receives *appellation contrôlée* status.
1944 The Allies land on the beaches of Pampelonne towards the end of World War II.
1956 Foundation of *La Société du Canal de Provence*.
1960 Opening of the dam at Serre-Ponçon.
1960 Brigitte Bardot hits St-Tropez, starring in the film *And God Created Woman*.
1970 A6–A7 motorway, the *autoroute du soleil*, links Paris and the South.
1975 Opening of the dam at Sainte-Croix.
1976 Completion of *Le Canal de Provence*.
1981 The TGV (*Train à Grand Vitesse*) links Paris and Nice.
1992 Treaty of Maastricht attempts to unify Europe.

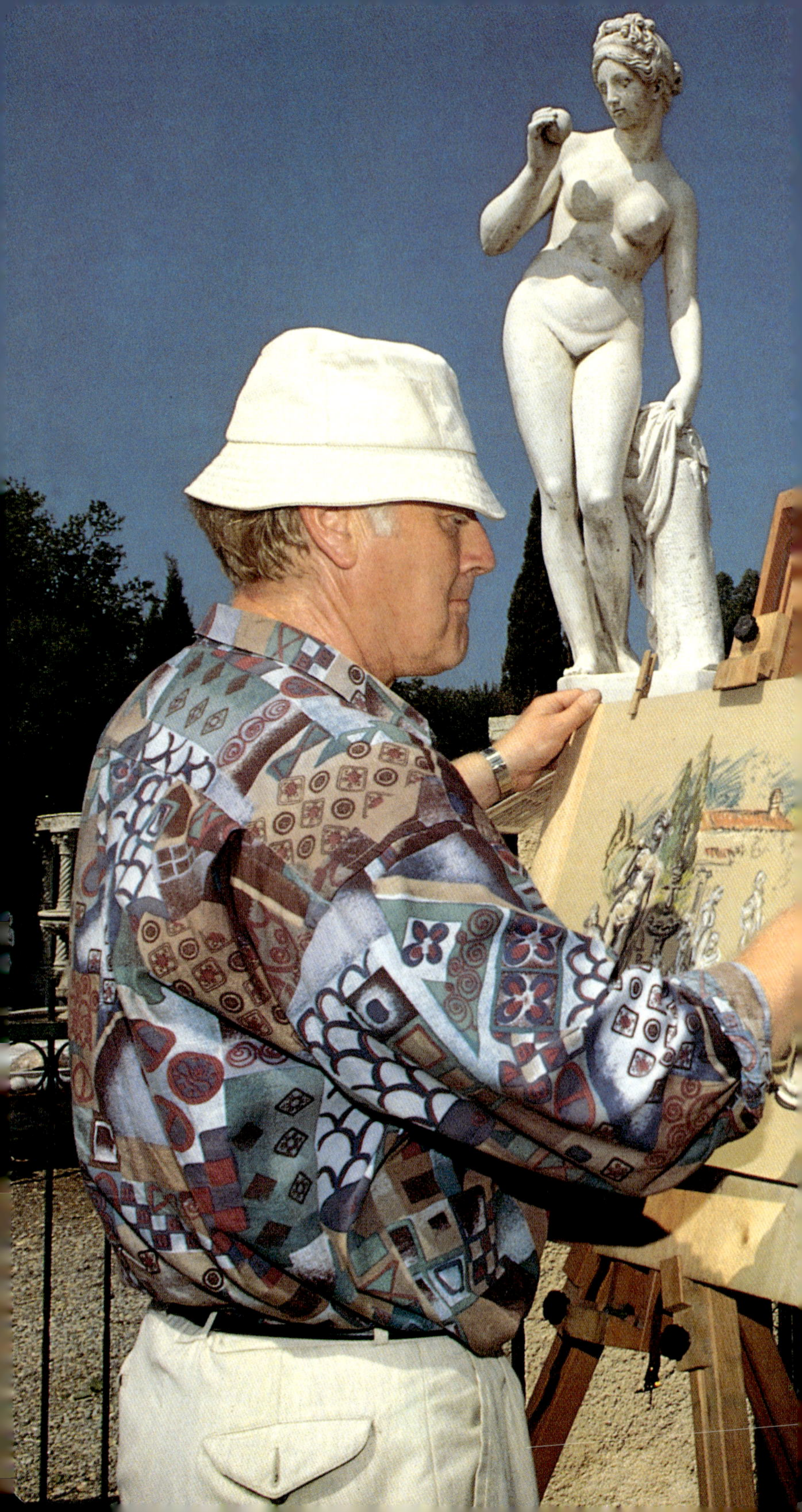

ROCANTE

Day Itine

The southeast corner of France is known as Provence-Alpes-Côte d'Azur and is divided into six *départements*, Alpes-de-Haute-Provence, Hautes-Alpes, Alpes Maritime, Bouches-du-Rhône, Var and Vaucluse. However, the boundaries of the 'real' Provence, like the ingredients of the 'real' *bouillabaisse*, are a subject of dispute.

The area covered by this guide is contained within the *départements* of the Vaucluse, Bouches-du-Rhône and Var. A car is essential – though any one of the itineraries could be achieved in a day by a good touring cyclist. The routes describe an uneven circle, starting in the north at the foot of Mt-Ventoux, heading south towards the coast, moving along the coast, then heading inland and finally back west towards Mt-Ventoux. Places to stay are recommended in the *Practical Information* section, with a price guide.

Most of the tours would benefit from starting before 9.30am, before the day really warms up. The tours are also shaped by the desirability of eating at lunchtime. I say this not only because this will be a good time to stop and absorb the morning's sights, but because in France the main meal is often at noon. This is also the time to find the local speciality on the 60FF lunch menu.

I have also provided choices for the hours between 2pm and 5pm, during the dreadful *chaleur* (heat) of the sun. As the ideal solution, to sleep, is not always possible, I have tried to ensure that this part of the day is in the countryside or near water. Most of the itineraries have an option enlarging the scope of the area, something too *special* to be included in the day, but too important to miss altogether. Finally, I have recommended a range of places to stay for each major itinerary in the *Accommodation* section beginning on page 84.

Preceding pages: Provence has a long tradition of artists. Below: ready to go

The Dentelles de Montmirail

The Vaucluse

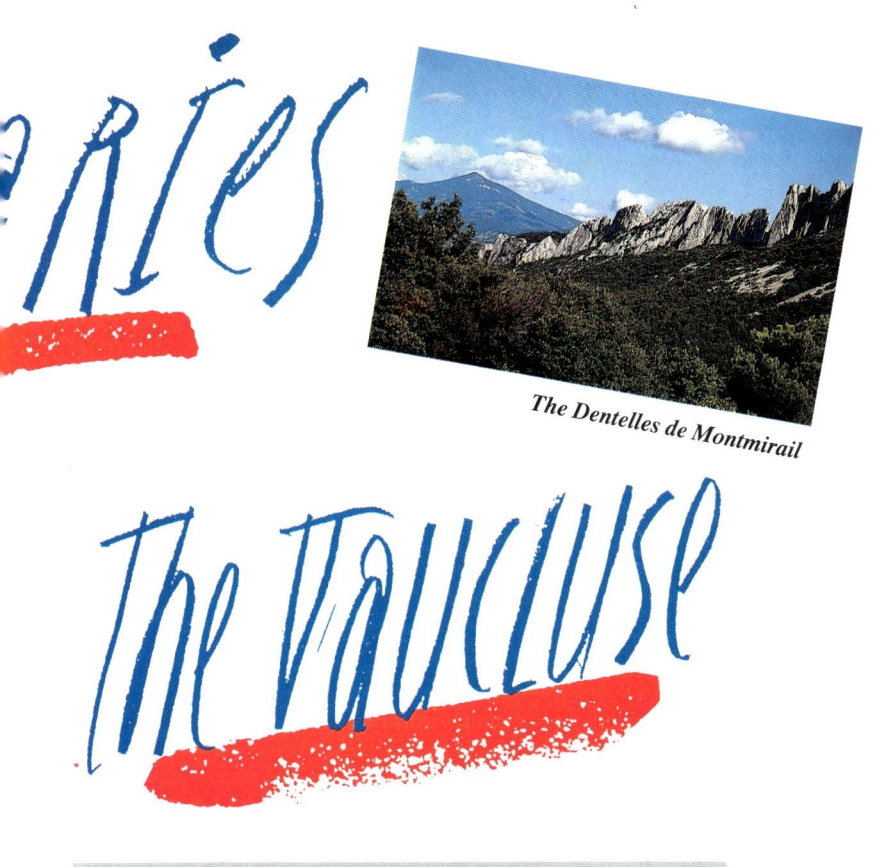

1. Picturesque Provence

A circuit of the Dentelles de Montmirail, taking in Roman ruins, medieval towns, perched villages, 'santons', the sumptuous fruity wines of Gigondas and the decadent sweet wines of Beaumes-de-Venise. 63 km (39 miles).

The **Dentelles de Montmirail** is a chain of mountains extending over about 15km (9 miles) of the **Vaucluse**, a *département* of great natural beauty known in France for the quality of its fresh fruit and vegetables. I would recommend **Bédoin,** nestling in the sunny pastures at the foot of the Mt-Ventoux, as an ideal base. Begin the day at the *Office du Tourisme*, where the *accueil* (welcome) is always warm and they are generous with local maps and guides.

The D19 from Bédoin to **Malaucène** snakes between the Dentelles and the lower slopes of Mt-Ventoux, with soaring mountain scenery opening out on all sides. The fortress-like south front of the parish church of St-Michael greets you as you enter Malaucène; in summer the people of the town like to sit on the cool stone bench at the base of this wall. As the gateway to the Alpine north face of the Mt-Ventoux, Malaucène is a busy town, but time can be better spent at our main morning destination **Vaison-la-Romaine**.

The D938 leaves Malaucène in the shade of a long avenue of trees and before long the medieval quarter of Vaison comes into view,

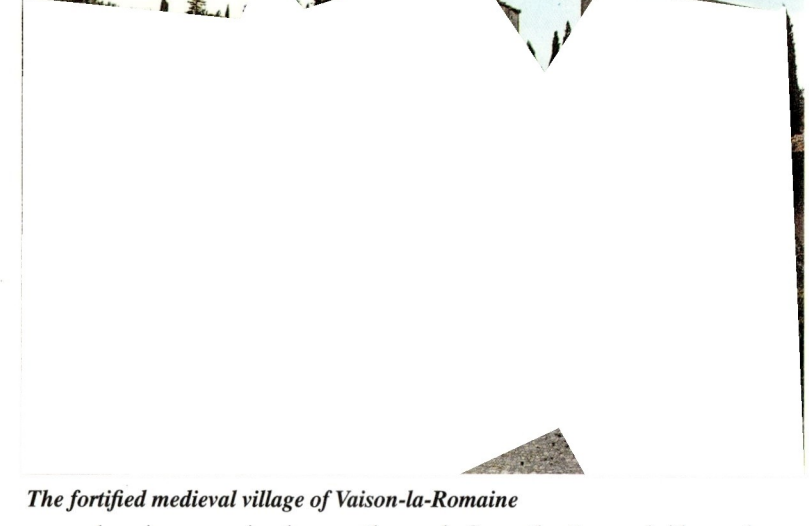

The fortified medieval village of Vaison-la-Romaine

hanging precariously over the road. Cross the Roman bridge and leave your car in the large space in the town centre. From here Vaison is easily explored on foot.

The town splits into two distinct parts, separated by the River Ouvèze. On one side are the Roman and present day towns, on the other the medieval town and traces of an earlier Celtic occupation. The main Roman site known as the **Quartier de Puymin** (entrance opposite the Tourist Office) with its museum, ancient theatre and large villa is magnificent and should not be missed. It is in my view far more impressive than the celebrated Roman site at Glanum just outside St-Remy. Contemporary accounts described it as the *urbs opulentissima* and one can imagine this was justified.

A 5-minute walk down the Grand Rue and back across the Roman bridge brings you to the heavily fortified medieval village surmounted by its ruined castle. The maze of streets contains a number of craft shops and an interesting 17th-century hotel. The lanes are rewarding to explore, but first turn left past the fountain under the Porte Vielle-Rue de l'Horloge and follow Rue d'Eglise past a fine row of cottages until you come to Le Planet. The view from here should please most people. From here Rue de Charite leads up to the ruined castle. As the castle regrettably cannot be visited the climb should only be attempted by those not satisfied by the view below.

Back in the main town Place Montfort – swamped by a market on Tuesday – is lined by *brasseries* on one side and is a good place to have a beer or perhaps a cup of tea at **Lanchier Avis**, an old-fashioned *salon de thé* on the corner of the square below the Hôtel des Lis. Afterwards, for all but the most ardent fan of Roman history, it is probably time to leave Vaison. All the better if it is

Well-proportioned Roman, Vaison

not yet 12.30pm because the question of lunch can be perfectly resolved in **Seguret,** your next destination.

Leave Vaison on the D977 (direction Carpentras), and after 5km (3 miles) turn off onto the D88 (direction Seguret). The exits from Vaison are not entirely clear and if you find yourself on the D975, direction Orange, don't worry – continue to Roaix, take the D7 on your left which crosses the River Ouvèze and go straight across the D977 onto the D88 to Seguret. This is what the French call a *route du vin*, literally a wine-road, and you will see on all sides the vines belonging to the area designated Côte du Rhône Villages, of which Seguret is one. As a general rule, the wines from these villages will be of a higher quality than a wine which is designated simply Côte du Rhône.

Seguret has two superb restaurants, **Le Mesclun** (see page 73) and **La Table du Comtat** (see page 84), and it is difficult to choose between them. La Table du Comtat is also a small hotel and is therefore smarter and more expensive; the owner-chef is a member of the exclusive order *Maître Cuisinier de France* and his cooking has a high reputation. Le Mesclun is a different type of establishment; each day they propose a new menu taking advantage of the seasonal produce, and for 140FF you can eat one of the best meals of your life. The choice is yours. If you happen to arrive too late for lunch, you can find a snack at **Lou Bàrri**, a charming *salon de thé*.

Seasonal produce is his business

Having said all this, to eat lunch is not the only reason to come to Seguret. Its aspect overlooking the Plain of Orange is the finest you could imagine. The village has a 12th-century church, 14th-century belfry, a superb 17th-century fountain, and not surprisingly is designated as a national monument. It is further celebrated for its Nativity play on Christmas Eve. The roles are filled by the villagers and handed down through families. This is a variation on the traditional crèche peopled by symbolic clay figures called *santons*, a feature of Christmas in Provence.

These figures can all be seen in **L'Oustau Dei Santoun** of Jean-Louis Romère, near the top of the village past the Cellier des Vignerons. His atelier contains *santons* from the two greatest masters of the craft, Paul Fouque of Aix-en-Provence and Marcel Carbonel of Marseille. He will be happy to show you the different styles of *santons* and discuss their history. Children love them.

Jean-Louis wears another hat as a wine-maker, and you should not leave without a bottle or two of his extraordinary red wine, made in traditional style from very old vines. In 1989 he produced only 1,200 bottles; it is a real *vin du garde* (a wine to keep).

Below this 'balcony' town, as it is sometimes called, you can see the town of Sablet, whose streets are built in concentric circles around the church in a fashion that is typically Provençal. Sablet has many picturesque streets and an excellent *caveau des vignerons* where you can taste all the local wines.

The next stop will be the famous wine town of Gigondas, a few kilometres further down the D7. However, real wine enthusiasts should look out for a left turn about half-way between Sablet and Gigondas and the sign for Domaine les Pallières. I can never pass this sign without being drawn up the old track to the Roux brothers' dark and winey barn. Their estate is perfectly situated in the foothills of the Dentelles and makes one of the best wines of the *appelation*. The best Gigondas are dense, ruby-coloured wines loaded with fruit and alcohol, and though some producers will advise you to keep them for up to 10 years, they can be drunk immediately, an irresistible reason for buying.

Gigondas is the Vauclusian equivalent of the one-horse town: its horse is the vine, stabled in the Caveau du Gigondas in the Place de

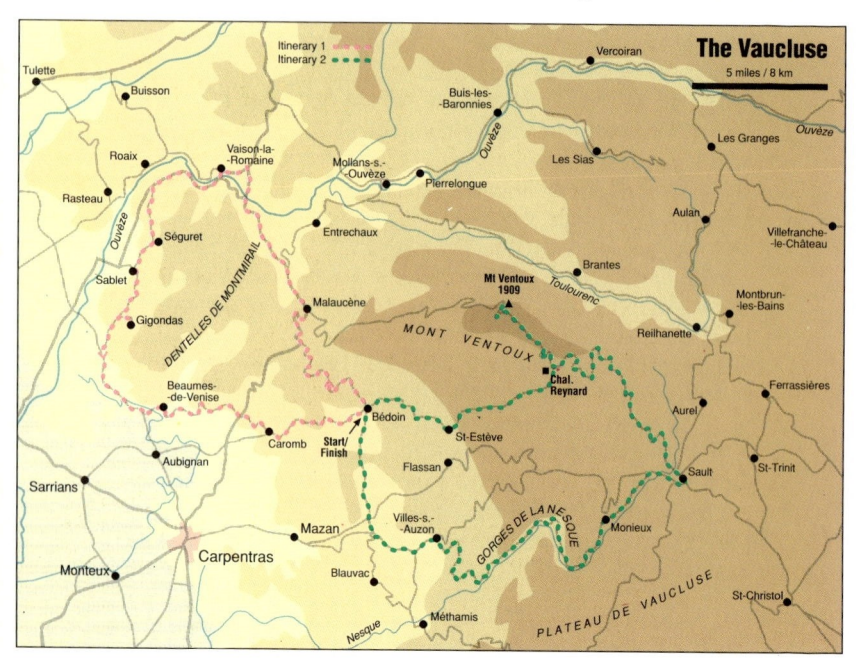

The wines of Beaumes-de-Venise are sweet

la Marie, where you can taste and buy the wines of 38 producers. The village is dominated by its church and the vestiges of the château built in the 14th century by the counts of Orange. Wind your way through the old streets to the terrace of the church for another great panorama. Gigondas is a starting point for many walks in the Dentelles, and though these may have to wait for another day, you could take your car up to the orientation point of the Col du Cayron (396m/1,300ft), facing the mountain peaks.

Over the ridge is **Beaumes-de-Venise**, only a 10-minute drive by way of the D7 (direction Carpentras) and the D81, which branches off to the left after about 6km (4 miles). Sheltered from the mistral at the foot of the Durban Plateau, the town is chiefly famous for its decadently sweet wine, the Muscat de Beaumes-de-Venise. The muscat grapes grown on the super-warm south-facing slopes attain a heady degree of alcohol and seem to soak up the aromas of the apricots and peaches which load the trees in summer. Locally this heady nectar is taken as an *apéritif*, a habit frowned on by purists who believe it should be exclusively a dessert wine. I'm with the locals and drink it at every available opportunity.

The red wines labelled Côtes du Rhône Villages also merit attention. The 1982s I bought from the Gigondas estate of Les Goubert are some of the best wines from the Southern Rhône I have had the pleasure to drink.

Domaine Durban makes one of the best Muscats and the twisting climb up to this estate (take the D21 out of the town, turn left immediately onto route de Lafare, turn left again where you will see signs to the estate) reveals another face of the Dentelles – now steep, terraced slopes looking like the green foothills of the Andes. It is a just finish to the day to have a glass of sweet wine in your hand and the Dentelles spread out before you.

From Beaumes-de-Venise it is a short drive back to Bédoin, via Caromb, or half an hour to Avignon, which is where tomorrow's itinerary begins.

Santons, Provence's traditional Christmas figures

2. Option: Mt-Ventoux

Mt-Ventoux; Sault, a village of lavender and nougat; the gorges of the Nesque valley.

This itinerary an option? Well, yes, to call the *géant* (giant) of Provence, around which so many myths and stories have accumulated, an option, is perhaps sacrilegious. The climb from the base of Mt-Ventoux to the summit at 1,909m (6,233ft), takes you from a Mediterranean to an Alpine landscape, through many transitions of temperature and vegetation.

The first recorded ascent of the mountain was that of the Italian poet Petrarch. He spent part of his childhood in Carpentras and later lived in Avignon. In 1327 he scrambled up the steep slopes in the company of his brother. If you have the time and the energy this is undoubtedly the best way to tackle Mt-Ventoux (detailed information on the routes can be obtained from the local Tourist Office in Bédoin).

The Ventoux is frequently included as a stage in the Tour de France cycle race and it was on these steep slopes that the English rider Tom Simpson died in 1967. Certainly this ascent is a *ne plus ultra* for a cyclist; the slope is unremitting and singularly unrelieved by bends.

If you don't feel energetic and the heat is getting you down, the summit can also be reached by car. From Bédoin take the D974 (direction Chalet Reynard, the base of one of the Ventoux's popular winter ski-stations). The summit is a further 6km (4 miles).

Though this area, known as *l'aire royale du vent et du ciel* (the royal place of wind and sky), is basically a mess, you will hardly notice, for the view is unrivalled. In summer the landscape below can be lost in a heat haze and a good case can be made for going up the mountain when the mistral is blowing the skies clear. Of course these weather conditions will have their own perils, involving a considerably lower temperature and a wind threatening to toss you back to Bédoin from whence you came.

Descending from the

Mt-Ventoux features in the Tour de France

André Boyer and his nougat

summit you can reach Bédoin in a circuit via Malaucène. However, it is better, and I cannot insist on this enough (even though it might take you more time), to return the way you came to Chalet Reynard. take the D164 (direction **Sault**) and from there descend through the stunning but little-known gorges of the Nesque.

These deep valleys are an outstanding natural feature and, after all, you have to go down anyway. First, though, stop awhile in **Sault**, to visit the shop of André Boyer Maître Nougatier. His nougat is made from local almonds and lavender honey.

Typically Provençal

The **Bar de la Promenade** (at the south end of the village *promenade* overlooking the plains, which in late June and early July are covered in beautiful purple lavender) is the place for a drink and a good cheap lunch. I remember sitting here in the early warmth of a July morning, with a large coffee, a *pain au chocolat* from Boyer's, Saturday's edition of *L'Equipe* (the French sports newspaper), with its reports from the Tour de France and before me the prospect of a day's cycling. What more can a man ask from life?

AVIGNON

3. Papal City and Vineyard Country

This full day's tour begins and ends in Avignon; the morning includes a visit to the Palais des Papes (Popes' Palace), The Doms garden and a walk along the ramparts. Leaving around noon, head for Châteauneuf-du-Pape for a good lunch and numerous wine tastings. From there go to the Pont du Gard, take a kayak down the River Gard and then return to Avignon for a promenade and supper. 80km (50 miles).

If you are coming to Avignon by car, plan to arrive early – by 9am in the summer – and park in one of the free parking areas outside the city walls. The most convenient are the areas by the Porte du Rhône (for visiting the palaces) or at the other end of the city, the Porte de la République, opposite the station. If these are full you can also park inside the walls, though here you will have to pay. The area within the walls is small and easily explored on foot, so taking a car inside is unecessary and should be avoided. For the out of town (afternoon) part of this itinerary, pack a bathing costume.

Avignon from Pont St-Bénézet

The town of Avignon occupies a rocky site at the strategic confluence of the Rhône and Durance rivers. The Romans marched past it on the Agrippan Way, following the Rhône valley from Arles to Lyon; later, travellers coming south would take a boat from Lyon to Avignon. The most celebrated arrival

Entertainment in Place de l'Horloge

was that of Pope John XXII who installed himself in Avignon in 1316, placing the town in the full stream of European culture. The last pope left Avignon in 1377 but the papal legacy is ever present in the city's palaces and its vibrant cultural life.

'*Qui s'éloigne d'Avignon perd la raison*', 'he who leaves Avignon has lost his reason', says the old Provençal proverb in much the same vein as 'he who is tired of London is tired of life'. Like London, Avignon is a city that inspires both love and hatred. Petrarch thought the city 'The thoroughfare of vice, the sewers of the earth.' We may have to allow for a little Italian bias here, but by all accounts Avignon had its dark side then and still does. John Evelyn, the great English diarist who wrote an account of his travels through Europe in the 17th century, was much impressed with Avignon: 'The walls of the Citty (being all square huge free stone) are absolutely the most neate and best repaire that in my life I ever saw: it is full of well built Palaces'.

The key to liking Avignon today, especially when coming to the city from the languorous countryside, is to be aware that in the summer it seethes with people and heat, reaching a climax during the celebrated **Festival d'Avignon** (usu-

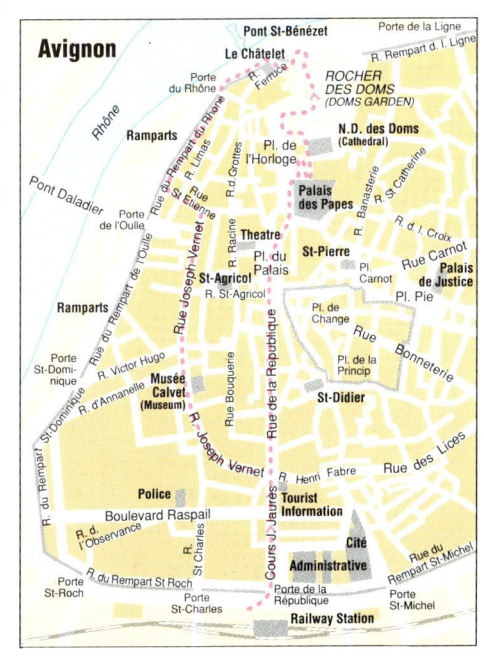

From the Palais des Papes

ally the last three weeks of July and the first week of August). The streets are animated day and night by street performers, musicians and young people from all over Europe. In my view, it is a time to visit but not to stay, unless you love the theatre. There is usually something happening in Avignon, though later in the year the mistral howls through the city, driving street life inside.

Avignon has a north-south axis running from the ramparts of the Palais des Papes, through the Place de l'Horloge, to the Porte de la République at the southern end. The **Place de l'Horloge** is the heart of the city; centre of café life and a popular breakfast spot, it is our first rendez-vous. From the Porte de la République it is a 10-minute walk along the Cours J Jaures and Rue de la République. Stop at the **Tourist Office** to pick up maps and guides.

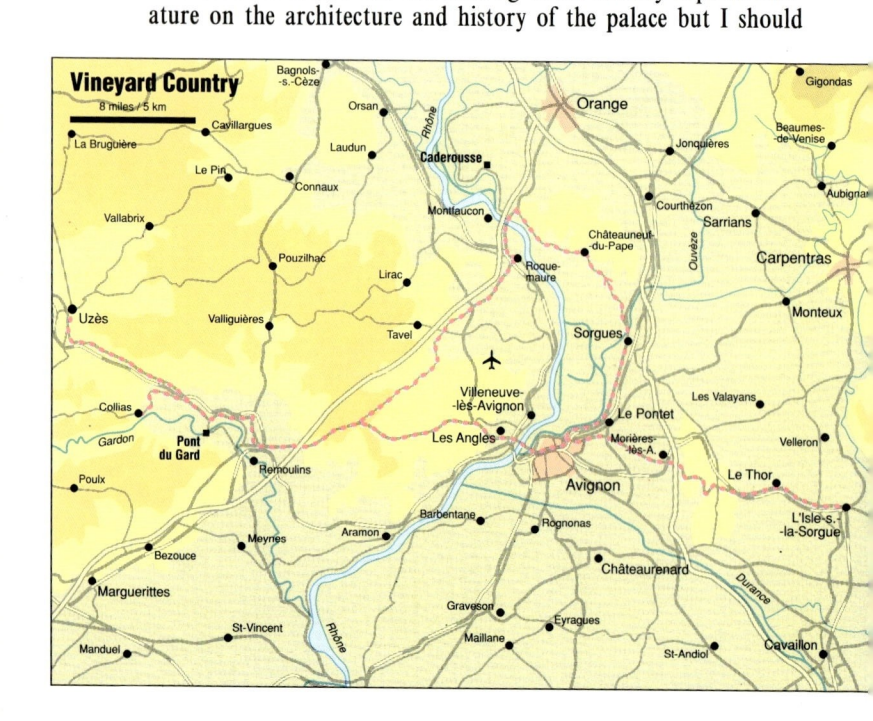

Visitors to the **Palais des Papes** (Spring Bank Holiday–30 June: daily 9–11.15am and 2–5.15pm; 1 July–30 September: daily 9am–6pm; 1 October–Spring Bank Holiday: daily 9–11.15am and 2–4.15pm; closed public holidays) must take the guided tour which lasts about 1 hour. I can add nothing to the already copious literature on the architecture and history of the palace but I should warn you that you will walk through a succession of empty rooms; only the magnificent friezes and frescos bear witness to the former decorative splendour. It requires a leap of imagination to picture the sumptuous luxury that surrounded the popes. Perhaps the sheer scale of everything is the giveaway; the shopping list for the coronation banquet of Pope Clement VI included: 118 cattle, 1,023 sheep, 101 calves, 914 young goats, 60 pigs, 69 quintals of bacon (a quintal=100kg (2,200lbs)), 1,500 capons, 3,043 hens, 7,428 chickens, 1,195 geese, 50,000 tarts, 6 quintals of almonds, 2 quintals of sugar, 39,980 eggs and 95,000 loaves of 28g (9oz bread). The kitchens are suitably large.

Leaving the palace walk away from the Place de l'Horloge past the cathedral and go up into the **Doms garden,** where you can recover your sense of proportion and admire the view of the Rhône and the **Pont St-Bénézet** – made famous by the song *Sur le Pont d'Avignon.* The bridge is a favourite spot for watching the sun go down. From the Doms garden you can gain access to the walk along the ramparts, which lead down to Le Châtelet, a small fortress defending the Pont St-Bénézet. The ramparts, built in the time of the popes, were restored in the 19th century but are only half their original size as the restorers were unfortunately unable to excavate the moat that surrounded them.

Vines and remains at Châteauneuf

From Le Châtelet follow the ramparts as far as you wish and then turn up one of the side streets and make your way back to Place de l'Horloge. The more expensive shops – furniture, clothing, jewellery – are located on this side of the main axis and the markets and larger stores on the other side. For the moment, however, postpone ideas of shopping, locate the car and set off on the road to **Châteauneuf-du-Pape**.

Once on the ring road, follow signs for Orange and Carpentras. At the first major junction take the left filter onto the N7 (direction Sorgues and Orange). The road crosses the River Ouvèze and shortly afterwards you will see the D17, the first turning for Châteauneuf. I prefer to ignore the D17 and go on to the D192, for this road winds through a small plain of vineyards to the east, slowly revealing Châteauneuf in the distance. The D192 comes to a crossroads where you are faced with a no-entry sign; in fact, you can use this road to gain access to the car park on the right. From here it is a short walk up the hill to the **Place de la Fontaine**, the

Pont du Gard...

centre of the village.

The history of Châteauneuf is indissolubly linked with that of Avignon and the 14th-century popes. The château looming over the village, greatly damaged during World War II, was built by the popes as a retreat and summer residence.

The popes are also credited with stirring wider interest in the wines of Châteauneuf. In his story *La Mule du Pape* in *Lettres de Mon Moulin*, Alphonse Daudet wrote of the Avignon pope who every Sunday after vespers rode 12km (7.4 miles) out to the plain around Châteauneuf to survey the progress of the vines he had planted *lui-même* (himself), and would pass the afternoon in the sun drinking a bottle of local wine – 'that excellent wine, the colour of rubies, which from then on would be called the Châteauneuf-du-Pape'. The wine is now famous, there are at least 50 major producers and most of them have a *cave* in the village – more of which after lunch.

The restaurant **Mule-du-Pape** (see page 74) on the corner of the Place de la Fontaine is a Châteauneuf institution. Upstairs, in the *Restaurant Gastronomique*, it provides serious food with a Provençal accent, downstairs and on the terrace it specialises in family cooking where the suggestion of the day might be an *aïoli* or a *soupe au pistou*.

After lunch there are a number of options: a walk up to the château, a *dégustation* (wine tasting) or a visit to the interesting wine museum on the premises of the firm Père Anselme. If this is not to your taste then there is an excellent municipal swimming pool close to the car park.

Not much later than 3pm you should turn your thoughts to the magnificent **Pont du Gard**. The journey is about 35km (20 miles), leaving on the D17 (direction Orange), and then turning left onto the D976 (direction Roquemaure). Continue in the direction of Remoulins, from where the Pont du Gard is signposted. You are now in the *département* of the Gard, which lies outside the present day boundaries of the politico-economic region of Provence. However, for the purposes of this guide, it can easily be argued that the Pont du Gard, as a great Roman construction, is within the context of a larger notion of Provence; certainly it would be a shame to miss it.

The Pont du Gard is an aqueduct spanning the Gard valley. It is the only substantial remains of a system built to carry water the 50km (30 miles) to Nîmes from a spring near Uzès; it has been cal-

... and friend

culated that its daily flow was 200 million litres (44 million gallons). To me this is an extraordinary tribute to the quality of Roman civilisation.

To see the Pont in the conventional mannner, follow the signs to the car park and walk up. A road bridge was added in the 18th century, enabling you to cross the river under the aqueduct. This in itself is impressive. You can also scramble up the hill to the top of the aqueduct, and at one time you could actually walk across, as the channel was covered to keep the water clean (recently it has been closed for repairs). It is a giddying exercise at the best of times; I like the small notices warning you to take care when the wind is strong.

An alternative is to view it from a kayak. These can be picked up at Collias – ignore signs for the Pont du Gard and continue on the D981 until you reach the D112 (direction Collias); just before Collias turn left down a narrow lane to the river following signs to **Kayak Vert**.

The trip downstream takes about 90 minutes, if you don't get distracted by the beaches and swimming spots, and allow half an hour to get back to the car. Kayak Vert have a courtesy bus from a point just below the bridge. There is no finer or more appropriate way to see the Pont du Gard – built by the Romans to satisfy their vast appetite and love for water – than from the water itself, floating round a bend in the river.

The journey back to Avignon is quickly done, via Remoulins and the N100 to Villeneuve-lès-Avignon. If you have any energy left this is the time to do some shopping.

If you have an extra day in Avignon and it happens to be a Saturday or Sunday, you are within easy reach of two of the best markets in Provence. On Saturday the lovely town of **Uzès** is buried under piles of the best fresh produce, olive oils, soaps and fabrics, and hums with activity (leave Avignon as though returning to the Pont du Gard and continue on the D981 to Uzès). Sunday is the day to visit the famous antique and flea market in **L'Ile-sur-la-Sorgue**, a cool watery town to the east of Avignon (along the N100).

Souvenirs of the bridge

ARLES

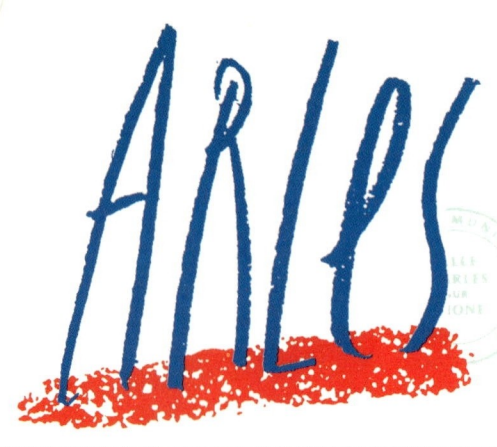

4. Roman Morning, Rural Afternoon

A jam-packed morning exploring Arles' Roman, medieval and folkloric legacy followed by lunch at the nearby Bistro du Paradou. The afternoon is spent buying olive oil from Le Moulin de Maître Cornille; and driving through the Alpilles to the Cathédrale d'Images and St-Remy. Evening spent in Les Baux. 55 km (34 miles).

Arles' Roman arena

The history of **Arles** and much of its character today was shaped by one major factor: it is situated at the head of the Rhône delta on the route linking Italy with Spain. When Rome came into possession of Spain after the defeat of the Carthaginians, Arles became a key strategic town, linking east and west with the valley of the Rhône.

Its vast arena (*amphithéâtre*) is the most potent witness to that time. While it is worth a visit, you may find this arrangement of huge blocks of stone leaves you unmoved; but go there the day of the bullfight and it will be a different story. All great stadiums are brought alive by the roar of the crowd. The bullfight is one of the great events in Arles and a reminder of its links with Spain.

The other remarkable feature of Arles is the survival of its folk culture, seen in the costumes worn by the Arlesian women. This may lead people to suppose that Arles is the town most representative of Provence, when, in reality, it

Arlesian folk costume

is something of a town apart, shaped primarily by its links with Spain and the Camargue.

I like to park on the Boulevard des Lices in the centre of Arles. You will find it by following signs to the Tourist Office. However, if you are coming from north of Arles on the N570 it is better to park near the Place La Martine or along the river. From here it is a 10-minute walk to the centre of town. On market days parking is more difficult.

Arles has a good system of *forfaits* (inclusive packages) for visiting the museums and monuments. Though I don't propose you visit all the sites it is convenient to buy the *visite générale*. You can buy the ticket at the Muséon Arlaten in the Rue de la République.

I am not a great recommender of museums, but the **Muséon Arlaten** (October–Easter: daily 9am–noon and 2–5.45pm; Easter–end September: daily 9am–noon and 2–7pm) is an exception. Founded by the great poet Frédéric Mistral, its theme is that of his life's work, a celebration of the people and the traditional ways of life in the South of France – you will notice that every town has its Rue Frédéric Mistral. As you wander through creaking rooms devoted to furniture, religious legends, *santons*, Provençal customs (for example, the female habit of carrying blessed peach stones to guard against bad luck) costumes, tools and *tableaux* of typical scenes and dramas, you will feel you have stepped back in time, a feeling reinforced by the custodians, Arlesian women in traditional dress who sit crocheting in the corners.

From the museum walk back to the Place de la République where you will find the medieval church of **St-Trophime**. The tympanum of the Last Judgement in the doorway and the cloisters are masterpieces of medieval architecture. English writer Hilaire

Inside St-Trophime

Bullfighters' bar, Nord-Pinus

Belloc described these cloisters in his book *Hills and the Sea*: 'The cloisters are not only the Middle Ages caught and made eternal, they are also a progression of that great experiment from its youth to its sharp close.'

When you come out again into the sunlight walk around the corner to the **Place du Forum**, where Van Gogh painted *Café de la Nuit*. The Place, with cafés and restaurants and the famous **Nord-Pinus Hotel** where the matadors stay, at one end, is the focal point of the town's cultural life. I have spent days sitting here. The Place has two excellent restaurants; Les Vaccares and the Brasserie de Nord-Pinus (see page 75), but unless you are planning to spend the whole day in Arles you should postpone these pleasures – perhaps make a reservation for the evening – and go instead to the Bistro du Paradou for lunch.

Paradou is a 15-minute drive from Arles. Leave the town on the N570 (direction Avignon) and shortly afterwards turn right onto the D17 for Fontvieille and Paradou. There is not a great deal to Paradou other than this one remarkable restaurant, the ultimate French working man's café, where lunch with wine is provided at a fixed price. This is now 130FF (such is the price of fame), including a bottle of the house red wine. At the price I don't believe you can eat a better meal in Provence.

The pleasing village of **Mausanne** 2km (1 mile) from Paradou is famous for the quality of its olive oil made at **Le Moulin de Maître Cornille.** The Moulin is only a short way off the main road but the left turn you need to make, though signed, is easy to miss. The best way I can describe it is to say that the turning is 20 metres before the restaurant Ou Ravi Provencau (this is another great restaurant and I intend no disrespect by mentioning it only in passing). The mill is a first-class place to buy gifts; in addition to olive oil you can buy soaps made with olive oil, tapenade (a creamy paste made from black olives) and jams. The

Les Alpilles and the Camargue
12 miles / 7.5 km

excellence of the oil is said to derive from the age of the olive trees – up to 2,000 years (though many were destroyed in the freezing winter of 1956) – and the exceptional dry heat of this area, known as La Vallée des Baux.

Les Alpilles, a chain of hills 25km (15 miles) long and 6–8km (4–5 miles) wide, rise above this valley, a curious misfit in this otherwise flat area and therefore an ideal site for a stronghold such as Les Baux, more of which towards the end of this itinerary. From the shady streets of Mausanne it is hard to credit the existence of this rocky fastness boiling in the sun a few kilometres away. I would advise against venturing into Les Baux on a hot summer afternoon. You will see the crowds as you approach from Mausanne on the D27. Better to pass a cool half an hour in the **Cathédrale d'Images**, then perhaps go down to St-Remy, returning once more to Les Baux in the early evening.

Architectural detail

So, by-passing the village for the time being, continue to the **Cathédrale d'Images** (10am–6pm) – on the D27, one bend above Les Baux – which has been set up in the former quarries mined for a rock containing aluminium, named bauxite. In the giant caverns of white stone left by the extraction of the rock, images are beamed onto the walls and ceilings by 40 slide projectors, accompanied by music. The project has been brilliantly realised and the effects are stunning. The theme changes every year; in 1992 it was *The Doors of Europe*, 'a symbolic architectural visualisation of the 12 countries of the European Community'.

If by now it is late in the day and you are returning to Arles for the evening, you might want to go straight to Les Baux.

The olive groves are up to 2,000 years old

Santon making is a local craft

Otherwise **St-Remy-de-Provence** is a pleasant 15-minute drive from here (continue on the D27 and at the bottom of the hill turn right onto the D31). It isn't difficult to pass a couple of hours sitting in the bars on the main boulevard or wandering the streets, trying to resist the gorgeous fabrics in Souleiado's window. From here there are two alternatives for returning to Les Baux; either take the D5 past the Roman site of Glanum or, more interestingly, return the way you came taking the D31 and D27. You will pass on the left-hand side the workshop where Monsieur Bourges models his *santons*, and as you come over the brow of the hill you have before you the great vista of the Valley of Les Baux with Arles in the far distance. In the near distance is **Les Baux.**

The settlement occupies a prominent place in the mythology of the troubadours and courtly love, which flowered in the courts of the Counts of Provence in the 12th century. The ideal of court life was to live in accordance with a poetic conception of love which exalted unsatisfied desire – that of the troubador, and by extension that of the knight, for the Lady of the Court. A rather frustrating, if romantic, concept. The ruins of the castle built by the Lords of Les Baux, where this concept was enacted, occupy the highest point of the site. You will not be disappointed if you make the effort to climb to the highest point of these ruins. Below is the village of Les Baux, a mixture of restored Renaissance houses and ruins. Abandoned in the 17th century, it is now one of the most visited ancient sites in France.

To return to Arles, follow the signs first to Fontvieille (D17), turning left when you reach the junction with the N570. An evening in Arles is best spent at one of the cafés or restaurants in the Place du Forum (see my earlier recommendations), but if you are lucky there may be an event at either the **Arena** or the **Théâtre Antique**.

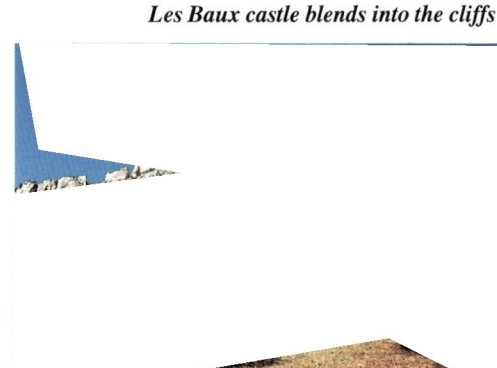

Les Baux castle blends into the cliffs

40

The best way of seeing the Camargue

5. Option: The Camargue

If you leave Arles on the D570 going south, you quickly enter a landscape of lagoons, rice fields and salt marshes, populated by cowboys, bulls and flamingos. This area, contained within the two arms of the Rhône river, is called the Camargue.

The Camargue is an entity the French would call *trés spéciale*. Though part of the *département* of the Bouches-du-Rhône and belonging to the *commune* (district) of Arles, it is a place apart, probably having more rapport with France to the west than the east.

There are really two separate Camargues. One is covered with rice fields, salt pans, stud farms and cattle ranches, and cannot easily be visited. The other is the nature reserve of the **Etang de Vaccarès**. Though containing an extraordinary diversity of wildlife, it is known above all for the flamingos (estimated at 50,000) who rest here in the spring and summer.

The main town of the Camargue is **Les-Saintes-Maries-de-la-Mer,** enshrined in Provençal legend as the landing point of the Boat of Bethany which brought Mary Jacobé (the sister of the Virgin), Mary Salomé, Mary Magdalene and, as one history of Provence has aptly put it, 'half the cast of the New Testament'.

Saintes-Maries-de-la-Mer is an enjoyable town to visit, above all because of the vast beaches – in the summer you should allow at least an hour to travel the 38km (23.6 miles) from Arles. Access to the nature reserve is from the D36.

You should also be aware that the Camargue has no tourist infrastructure, because living here is basically insupportable. The only people who tolerate the conditions are the cowboys, who rear the bulls, and environmentalists. The main plague is the mosquitoes. As a protected environment the Camargue has never been demosquitoed. They prey mercilessly on visitors, so take cream. The best advice I can give is to go into the Camargue when the mistral is scattering the insects. I think you will find the problems this wind creates with car doors more supportable than the bites.

Aix-en-Provence

6. From the Renaissance to Cézanne

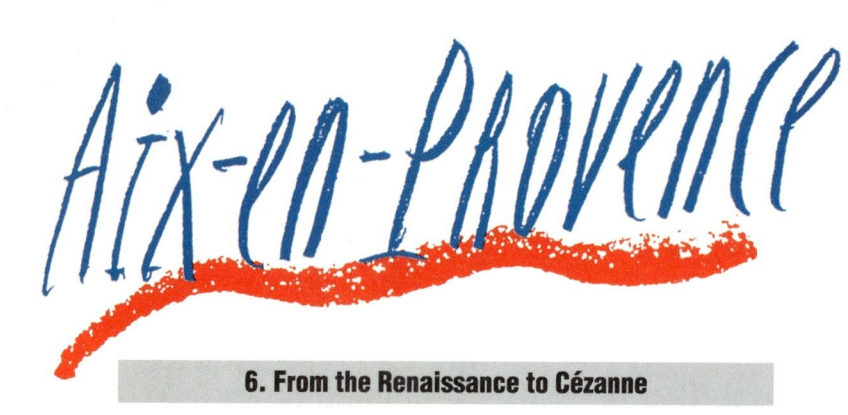

A morning tour of the elegant Renaissance town of Aix; lunch at Le Thelonet and an afternoon exploring Cézanne country.

The first Roman settlement in Provence was founded by the proconsul Sextius Calvinus after his victory over the Franks. He baptised it Aquae Sextiae, a name alluding equally to its founder and the thermal springs near the settlement. It became one of the most important Roman towns in Provence and a major halt on the Aurelian Way, the road connecting the Italian border with the valley of the Rhône. This is the site of **Aix-en-Provence** today. Virtually nothing survives in modern-day Aix from this period of its history. However, the position of Aix on the main route connecting Paris with Nice is a reminder that the main roads of Provence follow the paths of their Roman counterparts.

Door decoration in Aix

From the 12th century, when the Counts of Provence had their court at Aix, it developed as a centre of learning and the arts. The university was founded in 1409 by Louis II of Anjou. His second son René, who became Duke of Anjou, Count of Provence (known in Provençal folklore as Good King René), was an enlightened patron of the arts. He made Aix the focal point for artists in Provence, as Avignon had been a century earlier under the popes. The university and patronage of the arts do more than anything to shape the life of Aix today. The town is full of students and the annual festival of music is said to rival those of Bayreuth and Salzburg (doubtful).

It is relatively easy to

Breakfast at Deux Garçons

find your way in and out of Aix by car. When you reach the ring road follow the signs for the *Office du Tourisme* at Place du Général de Gaulle. The main car parks are located here, close to the fountain marking the western end of the **Cours Mirabeau**, named in honour of the Count of Mirabeau, the famous Mirabeau of 1789, who was the representative of Aix in Paris. This shaded avenue, with its four fountains and elegant buildings, every

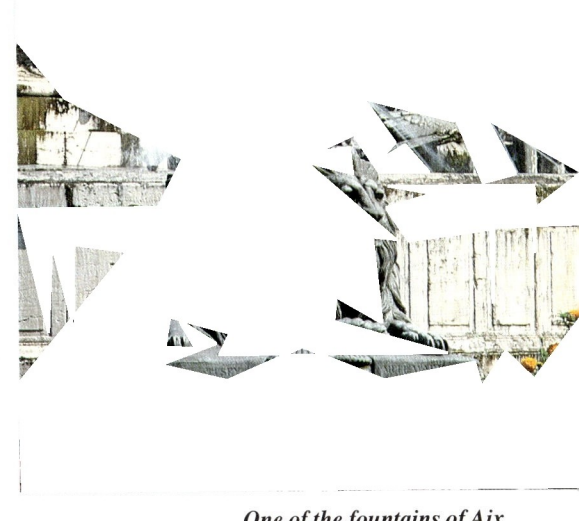

One of the fountains of Aix

other one either a café or a bookshop, is the heart of Aix today. It is a potent symbol of the sophisticated and cultured lifestyle of its inhabitants.

Days in Aix should always begin here, preferably drinking coffee in **Le Café des Deux Garçons** (no 53*bis*). Long-time meeting-place of writers and intellectuals, its interior is classic 19th-century *brasserie* style: wooden chairs, marble-topped tables, gilt mirrors and brass lamps.

The Cours Mirabeau was built in the second half of the 17th cen-

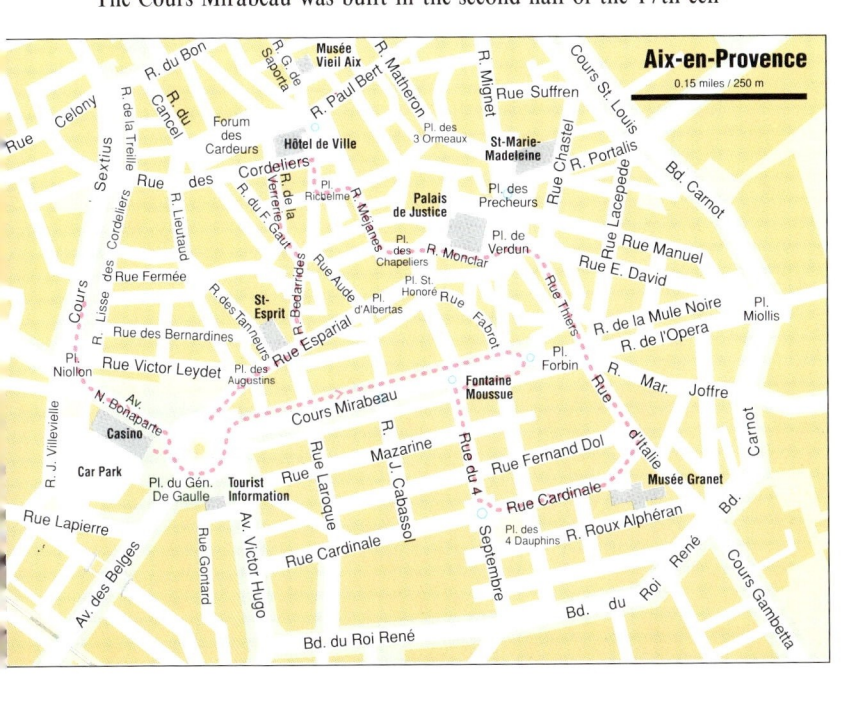

The decorative Hôtel de Ville

tury as a *cours à carosses*, a street for horse-drawn carriages, a symbol of the increasing prosperity of Aix, capital town of Provence and seat of the court of justice. The area to the south of the Cours known as the **Quartier Mazarin** was developed during the 18th century, on the model of an Italian Renaissance town. Fronted by the grand mansions on the Cours – *les hôtels particuliers* – the area rapidly became the new residential quarter of the wealthy who had lived until then in the old town.

One of the finest of the grand mansions is at no 38, Hôtel Maurel de Pontevès. Its facade superimposes the three classical decorative orders – Doric, Ionic and Corinthian – and is notable for the sculptured figures supporting the balcony above the doorway. The figures represent Atlantis, who in Greek mythology bore the weight of the world on his shoulders. As you walk round Aix you will see this motif duplicated on numerous smaller balconies.

In the middle of the Cours is a moss-encrusted fountain. Fed by a thermal spring it was originally called the Fontaine Chaude (hot), but is now more often referred to as the mossy fountain, Fontaine Moussue. From here walk down the Rue du 4-Septembre into the Quartier Mazarin. You quickly reach **La Place des Quatre Dauphins**, ornamented by a superb baroque fountain. This is the finest of all the ornamental fountains which adorn Aix.

Walking west from the Place along the Rue Cardinale you come to **Le Museé Granet** (Wednesday–Monday: 10am–noon and 2–6pm; closed Tuesday), the most interesting museum in Aix, housing a fine collection of paintings. Cézanne is represented by a dozen or so paintings illustrating the main themes of his work.

At the top of Rue Cardinale is Rue d'Italie where you will find the Confiserie Brémond Fils, one of

A long tradition of sweet-making

the oldest firms making the famous *calissons* of Aix: a boat-shaped confectionery of sweet almond paste blended with crystallised oranges and melons softened in fruit syrup (often apricot). In popular folklore they have attained the status of a kind of Host and are dispensed in church at Christmas, Easter and on 1 September, to commemorate the end of the great plague of 1630. Aside from all this they are very good to eat.

Crossing Place Forbin, you leave the Mazarin Quarter and enter the old town. This maze of streets north of the Cours Mirabeau is a shoppers' paradise. In the morning the market on the Place Richelme is a colourful sight. Later in the day this area is the place to come for bars and buskers and it is a relaxed alternative to the Cours. Behind the Post Office – an elegant 18th-century building that once housed the corn market – is **L'Hôtel de Ville**. Built in the 17th century it shows all the decorative motifs of the baroque style: pediments, friezes and the curling forms of flowers and fruit. Inside, the courtyard has a lovely harmony of forms and superb examples of that particularly French urban craft, *ferronnerie d'art* (art metalwork).

Towards midday in summer the temperature in Aix can climb high and the light becomes very clear, a phenomenon described by Charles Dickens: 'The town was... so hot, and so intensely light, that when I walked out at noon it was like coming suddenly from the darkened room into crisp blue fire. The air was so very clear, that distant hills and rocky points appeared within an hour's walk...'

It may be that Dickens was referring to the distant outline of the **Mont St-Victoire**. It is less than an hour's walk from the centre of Aix to the foothills of this mountain, and only 15 minutes by car.

Take the ring road as far as the turning for **Le Tholonet**, the D17, known as *'route Cézanne'*. Within minutes the boundaries of Aix are left behind and each bend in the road offers a glimpse of

Country life

the mountain. Reaching Le Tholonet you will see on your left a château, the headquarters of La Société du Canal de Provence. On your right a towering avenue of plane trees leads to a park. Continuing straight on, the D17 crosses a bridge and passes the Relais Cézanne where you will eat good country cooking and be charged between 50 and 100 francs. A couple of hours on the shady terrace will set you up for an afternoon in the *paysage* (country) of Cézanne.

Cézanne never tired of painting this area dominated by the Mont St-Victoire. He wrote to his son: 'I spend every day in this landscape with its beautiful shapes. Indeed I cannot imagine a more pleasant way or place to pass my time.' Le Tholonet presents a number of different options for passing the afternoon. Either you can adjourn to the park, a favourite promenade for the Auxois, or you can take one of a number of walks from various car parks along the D17 between Le Tholonet and Puyloubier. The landscape is fierce and hot in summer, recognisably the one Cézanne shaped on his canvases. Alternatively, you can make a complete circuit (74km/46 miles) of the mountain, via Puyloubier, Pourrières, the D23 (direction Rians), branching left onto the D223(D10) (direction Vauvenargues) and from there back to Aix on the D10. The area will take you through spectacular rocky landscapes, the vineyards of the Côte de Provence estates and give you a view of the north face of the mountain. This so captivated Picasso that he bought the château in Vauvenar-

Picasso's château at Vauvenargues

gues (unfortunately this site is not open to the public). For a complete circuit bringing you back to the Cours Mirabeau you should allow two hours.

You should be back in Aix in time for an apéritif and the *promenade* on the Cours, and perhaps supper at the **2G** (Deux Garçons) which is where you had your breakfast.

France's second city, Marseille

7. Option: Marseille

If you have found Aix a little bland, a visit to Marseille will quicken the pulse. Marseille, France's second city after Paris, is less than 30 minutes' drive from Aix-en-Provence (by way of the A51 motorway). It can be seedy, as every port city. The contrasts with the sedate splendour of Aix are severe, though the inhabitants of Marseille are supremely laid-back.

The appeal of Marseille is unconventional. If you are going to pay a short evening or morning visit, here are a few reference points. The restaurants of the Vieux Port are famous for the Marseille dish *bouillabaisse*; Miramar, in particular, is an institution (see page 76). Place Thiars, just off the southeast corner of the port, has restaurants and clubs open all night. The other main location for restaurants and bars, trendier than the port, is the **Cours Julien**, a 15-minute walk from the old port up La Canebière. It is the most famous street in the city, a symbol of Marseille in the way Fifth Avenue is a symbol of New York.

The best strategy for a short visit is to explore the area of the Vieux Port, then go out to the Palais du Pharo, on the spur of the port, for a fascinating view over the city. From here drive along the Corniche President J F Kennedy to the Vallon des Auffes, an old Mediterranean fishing port, where you will find three good fish restaurants.

On the quay

Along the Coast

In 1887 a French journalist investigating the British colonisation of the Mediterranean coast of France came up with an enduring headline, *La Côte d'Azur*. Though this describes the whole coastal area equally well, the littoral (coast) within the compass of this guide – Marseille to St-Tropez – is more generally known as *La Côte Provençale*. If you want to go further along the coast to Nice and Cannes then I recommend you buy a copy of either *Insight Guide: Côte D'Azur* or the *Insight Pocket Guide: Côte D'Azur*.

The three itineraries that follow have selected highlights from the Côte Provençale and each could easily make a day. The overall scheme is linear, linking Cassis and St-Tropez, two towns connected by 100km (60 miles) of twisting coastal roads; a magnificent drive on a crisp winter's day, a crawling caravan in summer.

In 1988 it was calculated that of the 20 million visitors to Provence, two-thirds came to the coast and the majority of those in the summer months. A quick, impressionistic tour of the coast can, of course, be made in the high season, but I fear the impression would not be a good one. My advice, if you only have one day in the summer, is to enjoy one good itinerary. Always have a swimming costume ready.

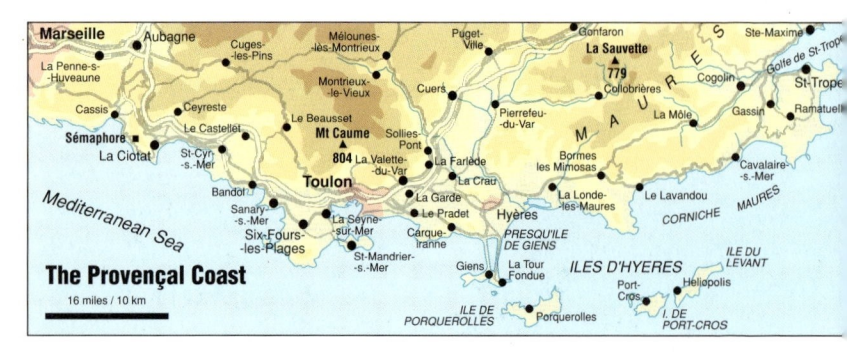

The Provençal Coast
16 miles / 10 km

Boats of all sizes along the Côte Provençale

8. Cassis

The old port; messing about in boats; a fish lunch and fine wines.

Cassis is 30 minutes by motorway from Aix-en-Provence; leave Aix on the A8 (direction Fréjus/Nice), turn south onto the D52 (direction Aubagne and then Toulon), take the last exit for Cassis, entering the town on the D559. Parking is never easy but early in the morning you should find a space in the car park next to the port.

The three things I believe should shape any visit to Cassis are: to swim in the wonderful waters of the *calanques*, to eat a fish lunch in the port and to drink the aromatic white wines produced in the surrounding hillsides.

The port of Cassis has a feeling of expectancy in the morning. Fishermen are landing the catch from the previous night under the careful eye of the restaurant proprietors and the boats that ply up and down the local coast are waiting to begin their daily shuttles. You can pick up a list of the trips on offer from a hut on the quay and then plan your morning over a coffee in one of the port's many bars.

Between Cassis and Marseille the coastline is a massive series of limestone cliffs, rising as high as 400m (1,300ft), indented with long, narrow channels of water – known as *calanques*. They were formed when the sea in-

Fish on the move in Cassis

'Calanque' boat trip

vaded the narrow river valleys between these cliffs at the end of the Ice Age. Some of them end in a small beach, others are hemmed in by white walls of rock that rise sheer from the water. The water has both a translucence and a density of colour that is astonishing. The cost of visiting the *calanques* depends on which ones you choose and for how long you go. The nearest to Cassis are Port-Miou, Port Pin and d'en Vau. Make sure you take a boat that stops for swimming. The *calanques* can also be visited on foot. The Tourist Office will give you a map of the *randonnée* (hikes) in the area, though you will probably find the paths are closed in the summer due to the ever-present fire risk.

'La route des Crêtes' to Bandol

Aim to return from the *calanques* in time for a fish lunch in the port. The **Quai des Baux** has a great forward line of venues: L'Oustau de la Mer, Restaurant le Port, César and Chez Gilbert, all make my first team.

If you are staying in Cassis and would like an afternoon excursion or you are moving down the coast in the direction of Bandol, you should take *la route des Crêtes*, the D41a to La Ciotat, along the magnificent cliffs of **Cap Canaille.** This road also has the advantage of passing the **Clos Ste-Magdeleine** where one of the finest white wines of Cassis is produced. The road twists for 13km (8 miles) up to the **Sémaphore du Bec de l'Aigle** – Eagle's Beak Point – where a vertiginous view offers you the whole of this unique coastline.

From Eagle's Beak Point follow the D40 until it links up with the D559 to Bandol. The town of **Bandol**, an endless seafront of boutiques and crowded beaches, you can safely bypass; the wines of Bandol you cannot. The town gives its name to one of the really great red wines of Provence and to one of the finest rosé wines in the world. The rosé somehow manages to be both light and full-bodied, the best of all drinks on a hot day. It can be hard to find as the best producers jealously guard their Mourvèdre grapes for the rich red wines with their complex bouquets of fruit and herbs.

Many of the producers are located near the medieval villages of

La Cadière d'Azur and **Le Castellet**; you will see signs for them before Bandol. They are more marked by the demands of tourism than the perched villages in the Vaucluse, but camped high in the hills they have the usual commanding views.

My favourite Bandol producer is **Domaine Tempier** (just off the D82 north of the city map). The welcome from the Peyraud family is charming and they always have time to give you a good *dégustation*. The last time I was there the sold out signs were up for the rosé so I compensated with a few extra reds.

9. Ile de Porquerolles

This is the largest of the **Iles d'Hyères**, three dreamlike islands where you least expect them. They are an image of an older Mediterranean coast, sparsely populated and densely forested, the beaches a dash of sand separating trees and water. The easiest and cheapest way to reach Porquerolles is by ferry from the **Presqu'île de Giens**, near Hyères. If you are coming from the direction of Bandol there is no need to go into Hyères. After the port of Toulon, take the N559 to Carqueiranne and cross to the Presqu'île on the isthmus behind the Plage de l'Almanarre. Sailboarders note: this beach has the best conditions in the south of France.

The ferries leave from **La Tour Fondue** every day of the year to serve the island's permanent population of 300 people. In July and August they run hourly from 7am, at other times check the timetables (Tel: 94 58 21 81). The service takes about 20 minutes and the round trip costs 70FF (the charge for bicycles is only worth it for mountain bikes as the paths are too rough for tourers).

The island is 7km (4 miles) long and 3km (2 miles) wide, well within the scope of walkers. The ideal mode of transport is the mountain bike. They can be hired from the village of Porquerolles (about 75FF a day), though demand exceeds supply in the summer. Before I leave you to enjoy this lovely island here are a few tips: pick up a map of the island from the Tourist Office and collect provisions yourself before leaving the village; there is no water on the island and no beach cafés once you leave the vicinity of the port. Finally, ensure you have enough time to get back for the last ferry – the taxis are expensive.

A sailboarder's mecca

10. St-Tropez

St-Tropez – the Vieux Port, the village, the Citadel; Pampelonne and its famous beaches; the hill towns of Gassin and Ramatuelle; the wines of Château Minuty; the Place des Lices and the Café des Arts.

A brief history: from time immemorial St-Tropez has been a village of the sea, home of fishermen, mariners and privateers. The port is an excellent mooring. In 1892 Paul Signac, the pontillist (impressionist) painter, came to St-Tropez and stayed, bewitched by the light, the deserted beaches and the little village of fishermen. Colette lived here in the 1920s, already complaining of the crowds. During World War II, on 15 August 1944, the port was mined and destroyed; 3,000 parachutists landed in the town, while the Americans landed on the beach of Pampelonne.

The 1960s heralded Brigitte Bardot in *And God Created Woman*, filmed here. St-Tropez became known internationally and its demise was forecast regularly during the 1960s, 70s and 80s. But today it is enduringly popular. Why? I think because it manages to be both a Provençal fishing village and port, and the very image of the *dolce vita*. The Place des Lices is the rendezvous for the local *boulistes* and where the celebrities come for an *apéritif*. The Baie de Pampelonne is filled with desirable boats and beautiful people; the sandy beach 5km (3 miles) long, is backed not by a concrete jungle but by farms and vineyards. Then there is the port and the nightlife. In this setting everyone has a chance to live out their dreams. I consider St-Tropez one of the great places of France, but in summer it needs to be approached with care.

A good day in St-Tropez is a long day. If you are arriving and departing try to do so before 9am and after 10pm. The N98 into St-Tropez splits into a one-way system as you reach the town; follow this until you reach Place Blanqui where you will see signs for the large Parking du Port. It is rarely a good idea to take your car further than this. The car park is a 5-minute walk from the **Vieux Port** and close to the Tourist Office, where you can find an excellent, clear map of the town and beaches. If you arrive before it opens at 9am you will find another office on the Quai Jean Jaurès in the old port.

Beach bar, St-Tropez

View from the Citadel

The morning is the time to wander past the boats that embellish the *quai* and to drink a *café glacé* in one of the famous bars, such as **Sénéquier** or **Le Gorille**. Never seeming to move, these boats are an essential part of the show. From the *quai* walk into the heart of the old village via Place de la Mairie. The village is a nocturnal creature in summer and you will find the shops only gingerly opening their doors at 10am.

Around 11 o'clock you should be thinking of leaving for the beaches, but first it is worth walking up to the **Citadel**, the old fort above St-Tropez. As you look over the tiled roofs and the clock tower to the Gulf of St-Tropez, it is easy to understand why the town has become such an icon of the South of France.

St-Tropez has two beaches within walking distance, the Plage des Graniers and the Plage des Canebiers, but for *le total* (total nakedness), you must drive round to the **Plage de Pampelonne** (from the car park head out of the town and after about 1km turn right onto the D93 *route des Plages*). As you drive along the *route des Plages*

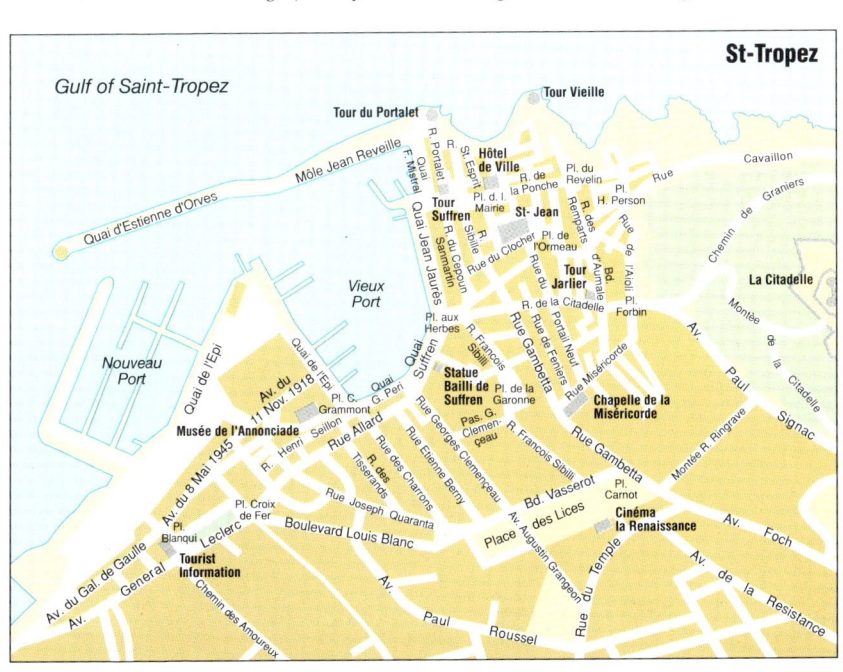

Tahiti-Plage

you will see signs for **Tahiti-Plage, Bora-Bora, Club 55, Nioulargo,** some of the famous concessions occupying the majority of the beach. A hedonistic day at one of these with a sun-lounger, parasol, the service of the *plagiste*, lunch and car parking will probably not cost less than 200FF per person. You can of course put your towel down on the public beaches and pick a concession for lunch. As a general rule the beaches are less crowded the further you move away from St-Tropez.

If by 5pm you find the charms of the beach are palling, or the heat is overbearing, the late afternoon sea breezes will be cooling **Ramatuelle** and **Gassin**, two hill towns behind Pampelonne. Gassin, perhaps the finer of the two, though less of a living village than Ramatuelle, has the advantage of being home to **Château Minuty** (on the D61 between Gassin and St-Tropez), a beautiful estate producing some of the best wines in the Côte de Provence. The white and rosé wines designated *cuveé de l'Oratoire* are very special.

If you can, avoid being in St-Tropez between 5-8pm when it is nicer to be walking in the vineyards of Château Minuty. For me this is the low point of St-Tropez's day – hot and crowded. One fine option is to have an early supper in the cool perfection of Gassin. However, you must be back in time to witness an important part of the St-Tropez experience: the evening promenade in the **Place des Lices** with an apéritif or a coffee in the **Café des Arts**. The other key aspect of St-Tropez is clearly the night-life, but to explore that would require another chapter and if you are in town for the whole day, you might just find it was *trop*.

Place des Lices by night

The Var

11. A Circuit in the Hills

A day's ride through forests of pine and oak, vineyards and olive trees; stopping to see the Château of Entrecasteux; swim in a waterfall and visit the market town of Aups. 60km (37 miles).

This part of the Var, whilst recognisably a part of the Provence you have been travelling through, is in many ways different. The first thing you will notice as you cross the A8 *autoroute du soleil* (the great divide in Provence) is the change in the pace of life; it is slow. This is a rural area but it is without the great agricultural riches of the alluvial plains which surround the Rhône. The forests of pine and oak are broken by vineyards and olive trees but not by endless fields of melons. As a result the culinary tradition is poorer, it is the *soupe au pistou* and the *aioli*, and the superb menu for just 60FF is harder to find.

Similarly the wine is much poorer, each village has a co-operative, but the wines are not of a high quality. Domaine St-Jean and Château Thuerry in Villecroze, producing good, sometimes excellent, red and rosé wines, are the only estates worth a special visit.

The villages are simpler than those in the Bouches-de-Rhône, the masons not having around them the tremendous forms of the Romans, who merely passed by this area as they hurried along the Aurelian Way from Frejus to Aix. But they have their own charm, their *cours*, cafés and *boulistes* and their superb *campaniles* – the structures of ornamental metalwork that adorn the ubiquitous bell towers and cage the bells.

Climbing up into the Var

Salernes is a good starting point. From the direction of St-Tropez it is a 30-minute drive from Le Muy (at the junction of the D25 and the A8/N7) via

Window in Salernes

the N555 to Draguignan and the D557. At first sight there is nothing remarkable about Salernes; it only really gets animated when the *cours* is filled by the market on Wednesday and Sunday. However, it is identified in France (and world-wide) with the superb work of its *céramistes*. At one time as many as 50 factories were producing *tomettes*, the small red hexagonal tiles which cover the floors in nearly all the older houses in Provence. The room in which I write has such a floor. Today the local clays are not only turned into *terre cuit* for floors; the superb glazes and designs of the ceramicists transform the humble clay into superb decorative objects – tiles for kitchens and bathrooms, lamps and bowls. You will see the showrooms as you approach Salernes on the D557; they are interesting to visit and great for presents.

From Salernes it is 8km (5 miles) to **Entrecasteaux** along the D31, which follows the winding course of the River Bresque. Just out of Salernes you will see on the right-hand side a series of pillars clothed in mauve tiling marking the atelier and showroom of Alain Vagh, one of the 15 ceramic manufacturers in Salernes. His passion is to clothe everything with tiles; his jeep and grand piano have already suffered this fate.

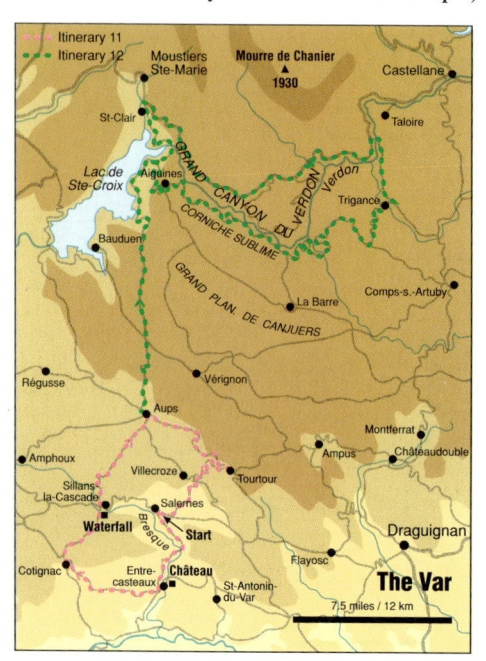

As you turn the corner by the football pitch the massive **Château of Entrecasteaux** (April–October: daily 10am–7pm; October–March: daily 10am–noon and 2–6pm) comes into view, bearing down on the small village of the same name. It was originally an 11th-century fortress, but the classically simple facade you see today dates from the 17th and 18th centuries, when it hosted among others the diarist Madame de Sévigné. Perhaps the most interesting part of its history is that you wouldn't see it at all today if it had not been rescued from ruin in 1974 by a Scotsman, Ian McGarvie-Munn. The restored château, now the home of the McGarvie-Munn family, has a light, modern interior, minimally furnished. Though interesting, you might think the entrance price excessive to view rooms decorated with questionable modern taste. You may prefer to contemplate the vagaries of history and have a beer in one of the bars opposite the château, before lunch in Cotignac.

The road to Cotignac (D50) comes up as a sharp right turn shortly after you leave Entrecasteaux. It winds for 8km (5 miles) through vineyards that just sneak into the Côtes de Provence appellation. You will see the big wine co-operative as you come into **Cotignac**. Turn left at this point, drive towards the main *cours* and leave the car in the car park on the left. From here you will enter the village at the bottom of its magnificent central *cours*, one of the finest in the Var, shaded by huge plane trees and surrounded by houses dating from the 16th, 17th and 18th centuries. Before settling down to lunch it is also worth walking up to the Place de la Mairie to take a look at the marvellous *campanile*.

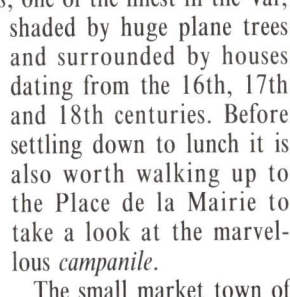

The small market town of **Aups** at the foot of the mountain of the Espiguières, one of the first spurs of the Alps, is your next destination. The D22 from Cotignac to Aups passes through **Sillans-la-Cascade** where, just under a kilometre from the village, the River Bresque falls 45m (150ft) over a cliff into a deep pool. It is a well-known spot and can be crowded in summer, but the walk is enjoyable and the water refreshingly cold to swim in. The path to the waterfall leaves the village on the corner of the road directly opposite the restaurant Les Pins.

Alain Vagh has tiled his jeep

Aups, as befits the chief town of the area, is a bustling place. In

Savouring the air in Aups

summer it is one of the few towns filled with visitors. In the winter it puts on another hat, and devotes itself to *la chasse* (the hunt); every restaurant has wild boar pâté and rabbit stew on its menu and the streets are empty. You will enjoy walking around Aups; the air is very pure and I always think the light has an extra luminosity. The last time I was in Aups I bought a few bottles of red wine from Maurice Chauvin whose *cave* is in Rue Marechal Foch. He makes an old style *vin du table*, fruity and natural, producing about 2,000 bottles a year from his small vineyards (he is one of the few remaining farmers who are licensed to sell their wine). For me he typifies Aups: welcoming visitors in summer but remaining true to the traditional ways of life.

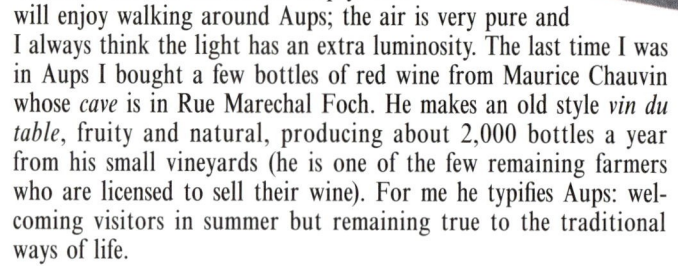

When you leave Aups, no matter where you are staying, you should drive the 10km (6 miles) along the D77 to **Tourtour**. The name of the village is said to derive from the Celtic word 'tur', meaning highest point, and if you go up to the highest point by L'Eglise St-Denis (towards sunset is the perfect time or when the mistral is sweeping the skies clear), you will be rewarded with a stunning sight. The village has built a very fine new observation point locating surrounding landmarks. The *place du village*, with the fountain in the middle, is a tempting place to have a drink and a meal. But if the day has not rolled on too quickly the last stop of the day is only a hairpin bend or two away on the D51.

Villecroze-les-Grottes has none of the obvious glories of Tourtour, though the park and the old village are certainly worth visiting: note the massive walls of the château and the fountain in the wall in Rue de France. Above all in Villecroze you sense life being lived to the full: the bars are busy (usually a chess game is going on, for this is a chess-playing town) and the *boulistes* are playing in the finely proportioned *cours*, bounded on one side by the village school; if you are lucky, the music academy will be hosting a concert or the famous rugby team will be playing a match. If not, the **Bar la Cascade** is a good spot for ending the day with a drink and a meal.

Villecroze-les-Grottes

12. Option: A Lake and a Canyon

The Lac de Ste-Croix and the Grand Canyon du Verdon. 120km (74 miles).

Aups is often referred to as the gateway to the Alps because the D957 leaving the town to the north climbs very rapidly into high mountain country. Within 30 minutes you reach the limits of the Var and if you drive across the Pont du Galetas at the bottom of the Grand Canyon du Verdon you are making your first entrance into the *département* of the Alpes de Haute-Provence.

The Grand Canyon du Verdon is one of the great natural sights in Europe, a savage slash in the earth, 21km (13 miles) long and at times only 6m (18ft) wide, compressed between vertiginous rock faces rising as high as 700m (2,296ft).

The instrument of this work is the Verdon River, now regulated by dams at Chaudanne and Castellane and flowing peacefully into the **Lac de Ste-Croix**.

A complete circuit of the canyon will normally take about three hours, depending on how many of the breathtaking photographic opportunities you manage to resist. I have heard that in August the volume of traffic can stretch this to 5 hours. If you are coming from Aups, the best point of attack is probably Aiguines. From here follow the D71, known as the *corniche sublime*. Built in 1925 to serve the new obsession with motor car touring, it is designed to render the full effect of the canyon. It succeeds magnificently.

From the D71 take the D90 to Trigance and then the D955 until the junction with the D952, the old Castellane road. At St-Clair, 33km (20 miles) later, turn left onto the D957 returning to Aups. This 99-km (60-mile) circuit will mark both the tyres and the brakes of your car, but I hope a more permanent impression of mountains and water and the great work of nature will remain in your mind.

The Grand Canyon du Verdon

The Luberon

13. Le Pays d'Apt

Perched villages — Roussillon, Gordes, Bonnieux; Cistercian simplicity and splendour; glacé fruits and the fruity wines of the Côtes de Luberon. About 70km (45 miles).

From a base in Apt the day is a roller-coaster ride through a small area bounded on one side by the Plateau de Vaucluse and on the other by the mountains of the Luberon. This area is generally known as the Luberon though locally it is referred to as Le Pays d'Apt.

Apt was a considerable Roman colony, on the route of the Domitian Way, the great road connecting the Alpine towns of Sisteron and Briançon to the northeast with the Rhône valley. Ten miles west of Apt, where the Domitian Way crossed the River Cavalon, you can see the Pont Julien, one of the best preserved Roman bridges in France. As you travel through this region you will be constantly reminded of past cultures.

The Luberon also has immense agricultural riches. Screened from the mistral by the hills of the Vaucluse it has the ideal climate for fruit growing and has made Cavaillon (on the western edge of the Luberon) into the great fruit market of France. If you enter the Pays d'Apt from the *arrière pays (*back country) of the Var you will remark the transition from endless forest to endless

Market in Apt

Mural in Roussillon

lines of fruit trees.

The town of Apt is in permanent anticipation of Saturday when the centre of gravity of the Luberon tilts east and the streets are filled with a maelstrom of marketeers. You will not find much to detain you on other days but it is a good base from which to explore the Luberon, as you can generally find a hotel room without booking months in advance. A coffee in the **Café Gregoire**, opposite the Tourist Office on Place de la Bouquerie, will set you up for the day.

Apt is famous for its glacé fruits in the way Aix is famous for its *calissons* and similarly they make a good present. You will pass the **Aptunion** factory on your way to Roussillon about 3km (2 miles) outside Apt on the N100. It has a retail outlet selling the many varieties of glacé fruits as well as other classic Provençal products. Shortly after the factory, you will see the first signs for **Roussillon**. The most spectacular approach is from the D227 (the third turning to Roussillon off the D4 from the direction of Apt), the village coming into view on a precipitous cliff which has lent its many hues of red to the *crépi* (cement rendering) of the houses.

The position of Roussillon is probably more spectacular now than when it was built, for two centuries of commercial exploitation of the ochre deposits have left it surrounded by red quarries

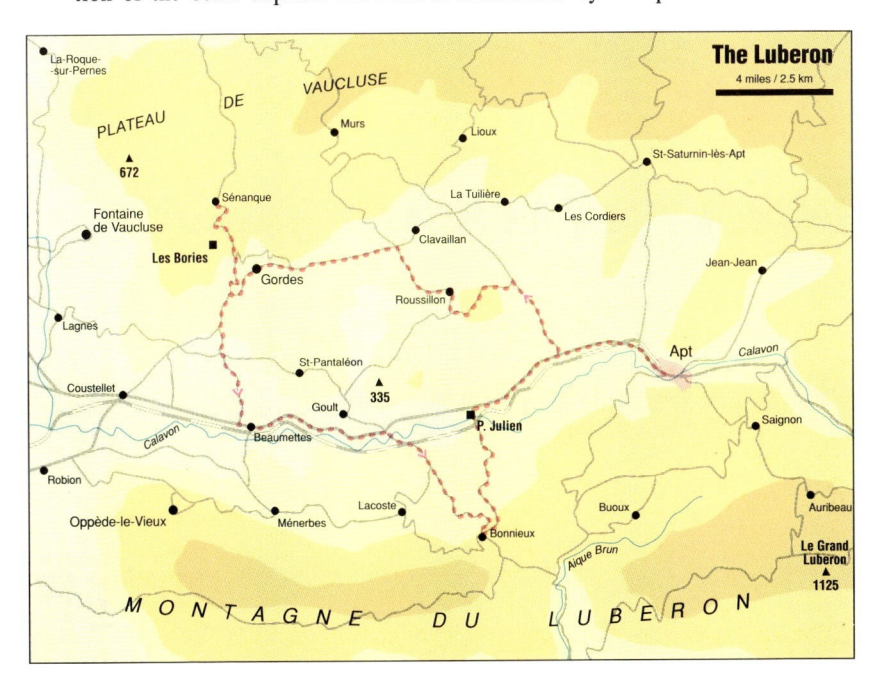

Enthusiastic visitors to Gordes

and cliffs. They can be explored by a footpath which leaves from behind the car park on the east side of the village, though these are best avoided if it is very hot or wet. You should not miss the huge panorama over the Ventoux and the Luberon from the *platform du rocher* at the top of the village. To the northwest you can see the town of **Gordes**, built on a promontory of rock at the foot of the plateau of the Vaucluse.

Gordes is dominated by its castle and church, best seen from the approach road (D15); but before entering the town you might like to visit **Les Bories**: you will see them signposted from the road.

Bories are dry stone huts built by marginally overhanging each course of stones so the walls incline towards a point, where large slabs of stone can bridge the gap, ensuring they are watertight. The *bories* were built and lived in by peasants, who needed temporary shelter to be near their flocks and crops. It is estimated that there are as many as 6,000 of them in Provence, normally isolated but occasionally found in groups, such as this one near Gordes. The *bories* are now home to a museum of rural life (daily 9am–sunset).

Les Bories

Archaeological evidence suggests that Neolithic man lived in structures such as these, which were rebuilt and copied over the centuries in a simple continuity of tradition, a tradition being continued in a curious way by the people restoring *bories* as second homes.

You can park in the middle of Gordes and, although it is crowded in the summer, this is probably a better bet than a hot walk up the hill. If you have visited the *bories* you will be in need, almost certainly, of a drink or two. The **Café de la Renaissance** in the small *place* behind the castle is likely to be welcome. Here, in the shadow of the walls, you can weigh the pros and cons of visiting the castle. The pros: the entrance is right in front of you, the castle contains a fine Renaissance fireplace and the views from the battlements are superb. The cons: the castle was extensively damaged in World War II, was scrupulously restored from ruin by the artist Vasarely and now exhibits a large part of his work. If you come out in favour of eating an early lunch in the Renaissance then that might not be a bad choice (details on page 77).

Before you leave Gordes in the afternoon it is worth casting an eye over the **church of St-Firmin**. Built in the 18th century it is remarkable for having retained its original polychrome decoration.

In the 12th century France saw the founding of the second great monastic order, the Cistercian, by monks anxious to return to the original strictness of the Benedictine rule. Their leader, St-Bernard, espoused solitude and silence and favoured architecture of simple, harmonious forms to facilitate contemplation. They began to build abbeys which would conform to these ideals and one of them was in the isolated Sénancole valley near Gordes.

The abbey of **Sénanque** (4km/2 miles from Gordes on the D177) in the Sénancole valley is the most satisfying building I have ever seen. When you look at it from the east over the lavender fields it has a perfection of form that is unforgettable. Even if you go no further than this point the journey will have been worthwhile.

The monks have now departed but the abbey can be visited (10am–noon and 2–5pm, except for the mornings of religious feasts). The restored building you see on the right-hand side of the valley is the refectory, housing an exhibition devoted to the life of the Cistercian order.

It is now time to travel to the **perched villages** on the opposite side of the valley: Oppède, Ménerbes, Lacoste, Bonnieux, whose names make up the modern litany of the Luberon. They have – along with the other villages of the Luberon – a turbulent history. Many were partly destroyed in the religious conflicts of the 16th century, but Bonnieux enjoyed great prosperity as a papal fiefdom until the Revolution. By the 1950s they were falling into ruin, ravaged by time and rural depopulation. At this point they were 'rediscovered' by artists and writers looking for an idyllic rural habitat, and the process of restoration began. Today there is hardly a house to be restored and though visitors course through the narrow streets the villages have not lost their appeal, partly, I think, because their sheer physical presence is more powerful than that of any number of people.

All of the above villages can be recommended for one reason or another but I have chosen **Bonnieux**, for the fine views across the valley to Lacoste, the steep streets bordered by grand *hôtel particuliers*, the **Musée de la Boulangerie** (bakery museum) and an excellent producer of Côtes de Luberon wine.

From Gordes, Bonnieux is about 21km (13 miles); take the D2 (direction Cavaillon), turn left onto the D103

St-Firmin

Up into perched villages

(direction Beaumettes), turn left onto the N100 and then turn right to Bonnieux on the D36. Parking in Bonnieux is not easy, but the nearer you park to the Hôtel César – on the right as you come through the village – the less you will have to climb. Opposite the César a cobbled street runs to the top of the village. Continue up Rue de la République and you will come first to Rue de la Marie, leading to the *belvédére* and a view out over the Luberon. Further up Rue de la République, at number 12, is the Musée de la Boulangerie. The museum has been well put together, although it is disappointing in some details: I would have liked more information on types of bread and the skills of the *boulanger*. As a friend remarked, a museum of the Marquis de Sade – who lived in Lacoste – might have been more interesting.

My great discovery in Bonnieux are the wines of **Château la Canorgue**. The château is a little way past the wide corner at the bottom of the village, along the D149 (direction Pont Julien). The château is archetypical Provence, fading yellow in a shady courtyard with an overgrown ornamental basin in the garden below. The wines produced are atypical in that red, white and róse are all good. The delicious white wine has a surprising length of fruit and the red 1990, already good, is expected to keep for 10 years.

With a few bottles of wine in the boot, you might like to finish the day by staying on the D149 to the **Pont Julien** and then, if the time is right, go back to the D4 and find a point where you can watch the setting sun turn the ochre hues of Roussillon to gold.

Château la Canorgue

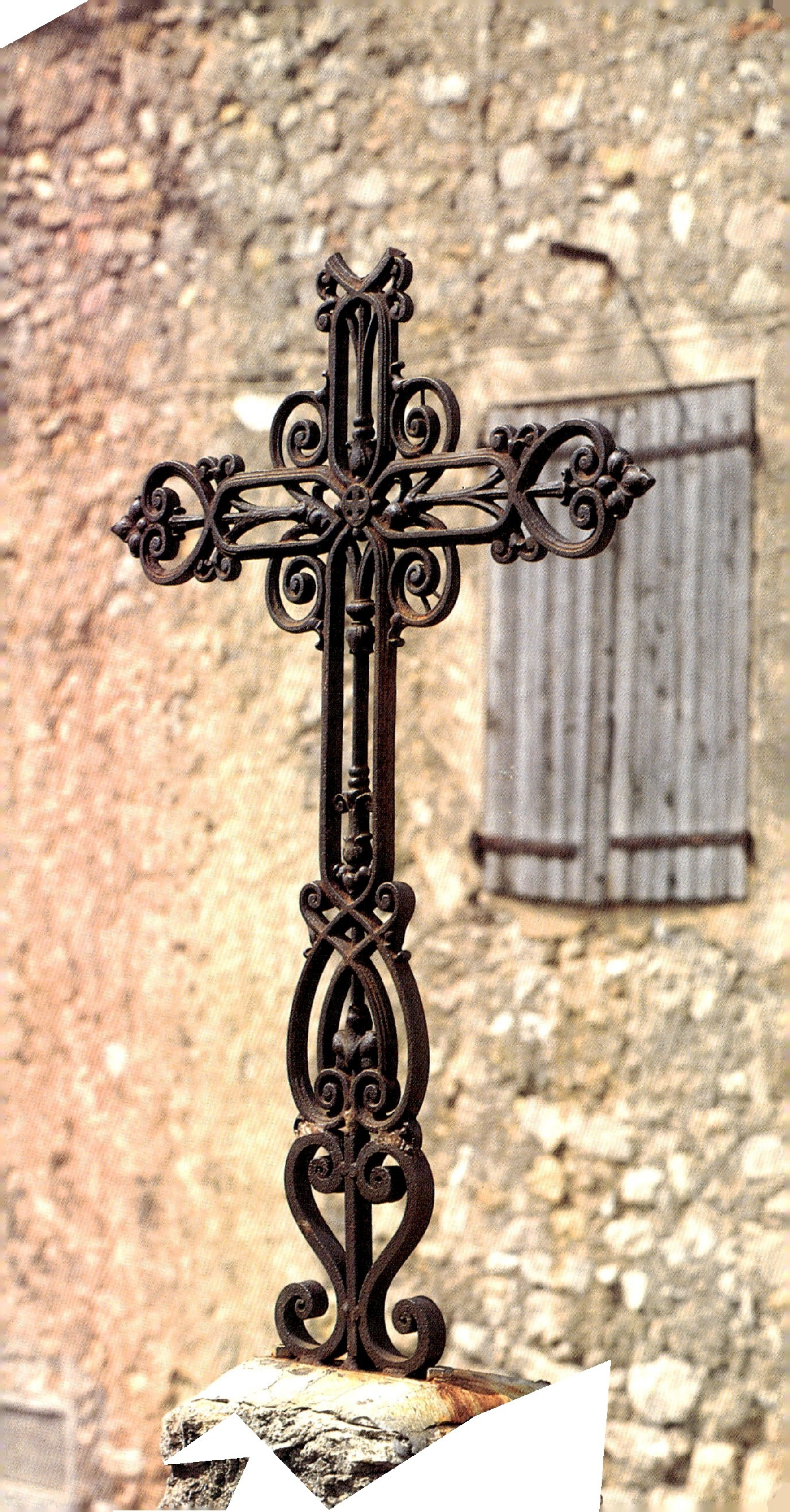

Shopping

Shopping in Provence is one of the best way of meeting the people who live here. I say meeting them because Provence is not a grab and buy place. Buying is often a slow process; whether you are a profitable visitor or a regular customer, the social aspect of shopping takes precedence over the commercial. In the *boucherie*, for example, the prolonged discussion of the relative merits of this week's *gigot* (lamb), takes precedence over serving the long queue and in the *cave*, the vintner is happy to sell a few bottles but he is often keener for you to share his pleasure in the wine and discuss last year's vintage.

Eye-catching display

Each itinerary in this book notes the characteristic product of a region or town, and suggests a place to buy it; *calissons* (a confection of fruit and almonds) in Aix-en-Provence, wine in Gigondas, ceramics in Salernes, olive oil in Les Alpilles. The excellent shops of Avignon are only briefly mentioned in passing, there being more important items on the menu for that day. A morning spent in the architectural splendour of the streets and squares of Aix-en-Provence is a shopping trip with an unusual cultural dimension.

Markets

Markets (see the weekly list at the end of this section) are the lifeblood of the small producer and the cornerstone of local economies in Provence. They are also social occasions of the first importance,

66

Market produce

when people come in from the surrounding countyside to review the progress of the *primeurs* and to bemoan the mistral, but above all to drink a pastis with their *potes* (buddies) and find out who has bought a new car.

Most villages have a weekly market that takes place through the year, on a day that is as fixed as the traffic jam on the *autoroute du soleil* on the first weekend in August. The stall holders will be local producers of fruit and vegetables, chickens and eggs, honey and *chèvre* (goat cheese); garlic and olive merchants (the latter often having as many as 30 types of olives – *noires aux herbes, farcies aux anchois, cassées pimentées, speciales apéritif ail-piment*); herbalists and the travelling *charcutières* (butchers) and general trades-people who move within a local sphere of markets.

There are also the great regional markets where stallholders travel great distances. These include the Saturday market in the town of Arles and the markets of Isle-sur-la-Sorgue, Apt and Vaison-la-Romaine. In addition to all the agricultural produce you can find superb Provençal cloths and *la faîence* (local ceramics).

ouleiado to take home

The markets are the clearest indication of the relative wealth and resources of each area. You will notice, for example, how the super-abundant cheapness of fruits and vegetables in the markets of the Bouches-du-Rhône diminishes as you travel into the Var.

Souleiado

The 300-year-old Provençal tradition of hand-printing fabrics breathes in one remaining firm, that of

In typical colours

Souleiado in Tarascon. Many of the prints are Indian in origin, brought to France at the end of the 17th century to decorate the fantasy world of the Court of Louis XIV, *le roi soleil*. The colours of the fabrics are derived from the hues of Provence; ochres, yellows, blues and greens. The Souleiado name gained international renown in the 1950s when Picasso and Cocteau adopted their shirts. Today it has the cachet (and prices) of a name like Hermès. Souleiado has shops in all the main towns and even in some of the smaller, wealthier ones, such as Gordes.

The Souleiado designs and colours are indisputably magnificent but similar designs are mass produced and available at much cheaper prices. Larger markets will have a stall selling these fabrics by the metre. Souleiado patterns can be seen all over Provence, covering backs, tables and bottoms.

Faïence in Provence

The art of shaping and baking clay has been known in Provence since the Middle Ages and has developed in a number of ways. One of the most sophisticated is *faïence*, the polychrome decoration of clay plates and bowls. Since the 17th century the potters of Moustiers-Sainte-Marie have held a reputation for being masters of this craft. You will find their work and that of other *faïenciers* sold all over Provence. Other products of this tradition are the tiles and ceramics of Salernes and the *santons* (clay figures), sold in many pottery shops but bought ideally from a small atelier, such as the one on the road from St-Remy to Les Baux.

Wine

Visiting private estates and farms to taste and buy wines is not normally categorised as shopping, probably because it is just too pleasurable. But there are many good wines to buy, particularly in the viticultural region of the southern Rhône. A bottle of wine is the most potent reminder of Provence you can have in your shopping bag. If I were you, I'd make that a case.

Market day at Apt

Markets

Market days are fairly evenly distributed through the week. They make such a difference to the smaller towns that it is well worth trying to make your visit coincide with a market day listed below.

Every day
Marseille-Noailles (vegetables)
Aix-en-Provence, Place Richelme

Sunday
Avignon-Porte Magnanen
Isle-sur-la-Sorgue
Salernes

Monday
Bédoin
Les-Saintes-Maries-de-la-Mer

Tuesday
Cotignac
Gordes
St-Tropez
Vaison-la-Romaine

Wednesday
Arles
Aups
Roussillon
Sault
St Remy

Thursday
Ramatuelle

Friday
Carpentras
Les-Saintes-Maries-de-la-Mer

Saturday
Avignon-Porte Magnanen
Aix
Apt
Arles
Aups
Bonnieux
St-Tropez
Uzès

More than just vegetables

Eating Out

What is the classic Provençal cuisine? As with all questions of this type regarding definitions of Provence it is hard to answer because the pages of the Provençal cookbook bear the same polyglot imprint as the rest of the culture; the cooking of a fairly impoverished region enriched by ingredients from the surrounding Mediterranean culture: pasta, polenta, *soupe au pistou* from Italy; carefully prepared little dishes, *crudités* and small vegetable appetisers from Spain; and *couscous* and *merguez* (spiced sausages) from North Africa.

The essential elements of Provençal cooking can be summed up as the use of olive oil, the dominance of vegetables, except in the winter, when the spoils of the *chasse* – small birds, rabbits and wild boar – dominate the table, and the use of herbs and garlic for seasoning. The latter is far less common than is supposed and I doubt if anyone would now suffer the fate of Smollett: 'I was almost poisoned with garlic, which they mix in all their ragouts, and all their sauces; nay, the smell of it perfumes the very chambers, as well as every person you approach.'

At its best Provençal cooking is a natural and seasonal cuisine, retaining the taste and texture of simple, fresh ingredients from the countryside and the sea. This was probably a revelation when Provence was first 'discovered'. Even in the 1950s cooking was generally much heavier, with a greater reliance on sauces, as fresh ingredients were harder to come by. As a result, the

Provençal fare

simple country cooking of a poor region was accorded an almost mythical status and exaggerated claims were made in its favour.

A good example of this is the *aïoli*. *Aïoli* is a garlic mayonnaise which usually accompanies a plate of cooked vegetables, always potato, carrots and beans, served with a piece of cod and perhaps some snails and a hard-boiled egg. Now this was clearly designed as a poor man's dish. The cod was used because it retains its freshness longer than other fish, but by the time it reached the *arrière pays* (back country) of Provence the pungent garlic sauce was probably essential. The vegetables would be leftovers from other meals. Apart from the village *aïoli*, a communal meal eaten in the village square, I run a mile from this dish. It has the unique property of filling the stomach with two mouthfuls.

Seafood special

However, eating out – and outside – is one of the great pleasures of Provence. I have given it generous coverage in the itineraries and I make a number of recommendations at the end of each section. Generally the restaurants I favour are those whose menus reflect what is seasonally and locally available. I am suspicious of *foie gras* in Provence. The most common regional dishes are listed in the *Menu Decoder* in this section (see page 73).

Breakfast in Provence is always a coffee and perhaps a *croissant*, *pain au chocolat* or a *brioche aux raisins*. As a rule, outside the main towns this area of the *boulanger*'s art is neglected in Provence and the pastries are often not very inspiring. If you find this to be the case, by midmorning you will need a *casse croûte* – literally to break the crust – otherwise known as a snack. Many cafés

Pizza maker

Ideal for 'casse croûte'

have a menu of *casse croûte* and this is an area in which the *boulangers* of Provence excel. The *roulot saucisson* is a very distant relation of the pink sausage meat wrapped in limp pastry that passes for a sausage roll in England.

Lunch in France is taken from noon–2pm; rarely will anyone want to serve you after 1.30pm, although the coastal areas are an exception to this rule in summer. The best value and often the best meal is the fixed menu, including a quarter-litre of wine, which is the French working-man's lunch. Usually it is no more than *correct* (right for the price), but occasionally there will be an excellent local speciality. This type of meal finds its apotheosis at the Bistro de Paradou in Arles.

The evening should begin at 6pm with the *apéritif*, a glass of white wine in Beaumes-de-Venise but more usually a pastis, a blend of aromatic plants and spices slowly macerated in alcohol and aniseed essence. Each brand is marked by its own personality: Ricard and Casanis have a taste of liquorice, Pastis 51 and Pernod tend towards aniseed. Look out also for Henri Bardouin, it has an extraordinary finesse.

One pastis and your stomach will be ideally prepared for eating, two or three and the bar will remain your habitat for the evening. The evening meal begins at 7pm and you will rarely be served after 9pm, particularly in the countryside. In the winter you can be pushing your luck after 7pm.

Another day, another bottle...

I have never eaten a meal in Provence without drinking a bottle of wine – not necessarily all of it myself. I recommend that you drink the local wine. Much of the *département* of the Vaucluse is in the viticultural region of the Côte du Rhône, and has some of the most famous appellations in France: Gigondas, Châteauneuf-du-Pape, Beaumes-de-Venise (the wines from these appellations are referred to in some wine lists as the Côtes du Rhône Meridionales as opposed to the Septentrionales of the northern Rhône). Here you will be able to drink very well and relatively inexpensively. The appellations of Provence begin below Avignon and continue over a vast area of the Bouches-du-Rhône and the Var (there is also a small appellation behind Nice called Bellet). Twenty years ago good wines were hard to find outside the small appellations of Bandol, Cassis and Palette, but today they can be found all over the region. Good to great red wines are in the Coteaux d'Aix-en-Provence, marvellous rosés and even some white wines in the coastal areas of the Côtes de Provence appellation. My only complaint about these wines is that they are sometimes overpriced.

The restaurants below follow the regions of the itineraries in this book, and many are mentioned in the text. Price categories are based on the following: inexpensive: menus up to 150FF; moderate: menus up to 300FF; expensive: menus above 300FF.

Menu Decoder – Provençal Specialities

aïoli: garlic mayonnaise with cooked vegetables and cod.
anchoïade: a purée of anchovies, olive oil and capers.
boeuf en daube: pieces of beef cooked in olive oil with bacon, onions, garlic, with red wine.
bouillabaisse: a wide variety of fish (at least 12), boiled rapidly in olive oil with saffron.
bourride: same genre as above but with white fish and served with garlic.
grenouilles à la Provençale: frogs' legs, coated with flour and grilled in olive oil with garlic.
lapin à la Provençale: rabbit cooked slowly in white wine, with garlic, mustard, herbs and carrots.
loup au fenouil: loup grilled with fennel.
pieds-paquets: packets of tripe cooked very slowly in white wine with onions and carrots.
soupe au pistou: vegetable soup with a base of basil and garlic crushed in olive oil.
tapenade: purée of black olives and capers mixed with olive oil.

The Vaucluse

Seguret

RESTAURANT LE MESCLUN
Tel: 90 46 93 43.
A gastronomic treat. Booking essential. Closed Mondays. Moderate.

Sablet

CAFÉ-RESTAURANT DES SPORTS
Tel: 90 46 90 24.
I love this kind of place. They put a carafe of wine on the table when you arrive, bring you three good courses and require only a few dozen francs when you leave. Moderate.

Gigondas

HOTELLERIE 'LES FLORETS'
Tel: 90 65 85 01.
2km (1 mile) from Gigondas in the foothills of the Dentelles. Good restaurant with terrace. Moderate.

Ready to start

RESTAURANT L'OUSTALET
Tel: 90 65 85 30.
In the centre of Gigondas. Traditional Provençal cooking, first-rate wine list. Moderate.

Beaumes-de-Venise

RESTAURANT LOU CASTELLET
Tel: 90 62 92 01.
An ambitious restaurant where, as the French would say, the rapport between price and quality is excellent. Moderate.

RESTAURANT LOU BRASERO
Tel: 90 62 90 83.
Located outside the village, follow route de Lafare. Open evenings only from 7.30pm. They make huge pizzas. Just to sit here in the shadow of the Dentelles is worth the 2km (1 mile) drive from Beaumes-de-Venise. Inexpensive.

Avignon

HIÉLY
5 Rue République.
Tel: 90 86 17 07.
Normally closed 18 June–4 July and Monday and Tuesday – except in July. Avignon's temple of gastronomy. Famous for its classical cuisine shaped by the best regional ingredients and wonderful wine list. One of my top five restaurants in Provence. Booking is essential. Moderate.

LA FOURCHETTE
17 Rue Racine.
Tel: 90 85 20 93.
Atmospheric bistro-style restaurant, also run by the Hiély family. Busy at lunch time. Moderate.

LA TACHE D'ENCRE
22 Rue des Teinturiers.
Tel: 90 85 46 03.
Café-theatre with live music at weekends. Good *plat du jour* for lunch at 50FF. Teinturiers is one of the most interesting streets in Avignon, and a key location for the alternative theatre during the festival. Inexpensive.

LE PETIT BEDON
(The Little Paunch)
70 Rue Joseph-Vernet.
Tel: 90 82 33 98.
Closed Sunday. Provençal specialities, another favourite. Inexpensive.

Châteauneuf-du-Pape

LA MULE-DU-PAPE
Place de la Fontaine.
Tel: 90 83 73 30.
Moderate.

LA MERE GERMAINE HOTEL AND RESTAURANT
Place de la Fontaine.
Tel: 90 83 70 72.
Sitting on the shady terrace overlooking the vineyards with the rich smell of garlic and flowers.

Arles

VACCARES
Place du Forum.
Tel 90 96 06 17.
The restaurant of M. and Mme. Du-

mas. The combination of traditional dishes prepared at the highest level, the wine list comprising all the great wines of the Rhône and Provence (M. Dumas' real passion) and the dining room and terrace overlooking the Place du Forum make this my favourite restaurant. I can't resist mentioning the *risotto de langoustines au basilic* and *la brouffado des mariniers du Rhône* – marinated beef cooked with anchovies. Booking is a good idea, particularly if you would like a table on the balcony overlooking the Place. Moderate.

BRASSERIE DE NORD-PINUS
Place du Forum.
Tel: 90 93 44 44.
Attached to the hotel, with a dining area on the square. Run by the son of M. Dumas. The best meal in Arles for under 100FF. Inexpensive.

Les Baux
OUSTAU DE BAUMANIERE
Tel: 90 54 33 07.
This is one of the famous restaurants in France and also a luxury hotel. Recently reduced by the inspectors of Michelin from exalted three star status to two star. I had dinner here recently in the company of some American friends and we couldn't see how it could be better. Expensive.

St Remy
LE RESTAURANT DES ARTS
30 Boulevard Victor Hugo.
Tel: 90 92 08 50.
Inexpensive.

JARDIN DE FRÉDÉRIC
8 Boulevard Gambetta.
Tel: 90 92 27 76.
Moderate.

Aix-en-Provence
CLOS DE LA VIOLETTE
10 Avenue de la Violette.
Tel: 42 23 30 71.
Considered to be the top restaurant in Aix. The chef Jean-Marc Banzo studied with Hiély in Avignon. The garden is a lovely, comfortable place to eat in the evening. Closed Sunday. Booking essential in July. Expensive.

COTÉ COUR
19 Cours Mirabeau.
Tel: 42 26 32 39.
A beautifully-designed relatively new restaurant. Classic Provençal cooking accompanied by and an interesting wine list. Moderate.

Make your reservations early

Marseille

Miramar
12 quai Port.
Tel: 91 91 10 40.
Expensive.

L'Epuisette
Vallon des Auffes.
Tel: 91 52 17 82.
Closed weekends. Moderate.

Chez Jeannot
Tel: 91 52 11 28.
The cheapest of the three places and open weekends, closed Monday. Inexpensive.

A roadside stop

Special at Marseille's Miramar

Along the Coast

Cassis

La Cadiere-d'Azur
Hostellerie Bérard
Rue Gabriel-Péri.
Tel: 94 90 11 43.
An old convent in the heart of the medieval town, with good regional cooking and panoramic views over the vineyards of Bandol. Expensive.

Restaurant 'La tonnelle des délices'
Place Gambetta.
Tel: 94 71 34 84.
The best cooking in the region. I have eaten a dish of langoustine with a 'spaghetti' of courgettes I hoped would never end. They operate a system of two seatings in the summer but you will still need to book to be sure. Moderate.

St-Tropez

La Pesquiere
1 Rue des Remparts.
Tel: 94 97 05 92.
Excellent traditional fish dishes served. Moderate.

La Marjolaine
Rue François-Sibile.
Tel: 94 97 04 60.
Good typical trattoria cooking – veal, pizza, pasta, and local shrimps. Inexpensive.

Lou Revelen
4 Rue des Remparts.
Tel: 94 97 06 34.
Fish specialities. Booking required in summer. Moderate.

Le Bistrot des Lices
3 Place des Lices.
Tel: 94 97 29 00.
Trendy, great ambience, music and great Provençal cooking. Moderate.

The Var

Entrecasteaux

Restaurant la Falaise
Tel: 94 04 76 60.
Overlooking the *cours*, serving solid Provençal cooking. Inexpensive.

Bar Restaurant des Sports
Tel: 94 04 60 17.
Located by the fountain at the top end of the *cours*. A delightful place to eat. Inexpensive.

Villecroze-les-Grottes

Bar Restaurant la Cascade
Tel: 94 70 63 13.
The village bar and restaurant. Inexpensive.

Restaurant Le Colombier
Route de Draguignan.
Tel: 94 70 63 23.
A short walk from Villecroze. Classical cooking which is even better now that it has a more regional accent. Moderate.

The Luberon

Roussillon

Restaurant Le Val des Fées
Rue Richard Casteau.
Tel: 90 05 64 99.
Considered to be one of the best in the Luberon; terrace looking over the Val des Fées. Perhaps too formal for lunch. Moderate.

Gordes

Restaurant le Renaissance
Tel: 90 72 02 02.
Good regional cooking. Also three bedrooms from 250FF. Inexpensive.

Chez Tante Yvonne
Place Genty-Pantaly.
Tel: 90 72 02 54.
Moderate.

Bonnieux

Le Fournil
5 Place Carnot.
Tel: 90 75 83 62.
All you could require for a good meal at lunch time. Shady terrace with fountain, cooking with a regional accent of a very high order. Inexpensive.

Dessert on its way

Calendar of Special Events

FEBRUARY/MARCH

Bormes-les-Mimosa
10 February: Grand Mimosa Parade.
Arles
Easter weekend: *Feria* (bullfights).

APRIL

Châteauneuf-du-Pape
24 April: Wine-growers' Festival (blessing of the vines).
Avignon
late April, early May: Avignon Fair.

Entertainment in Arles

MAY

May Day: Festivals throughout Provence.
Arles
1 May: Feast of the Gardians (the cowboys of the Camargue).
Aups
12 May: Festival of St Pancras.
St-Tropez
16, 17, 18 May: *La Bravade*.
Les-Saintes-Maries-de-la-Mer
24, 25 May: Festival and Pilgrimage.

JUNE

St-Tropez
15 June: *La Bravade* commemorating victory over the Spanish fleet in 1637. Feast Day of St John the Baptist.
24 June: celebrated throughout Provence.
Les Baux
Last Saturday in June: Folklore Festival of John the Baptist.
Tarascon
Last Sunday in June: Festival of *Tarasque*, one of Provence's best-known religious festivals.

JULY

Arles
International Festival of Photography and Festival of Arles (bullfights, music, theatre).
Avignon
Early July: Festival of French and American Cinema.
Last two weeks of July/first week of August: Festival of Theatre.
Vacqueyras
Wine Festival of local Côtes du Rhone Villages appellations.
Bastille Day
14 July: firework displays and festivals all over Provence.
Vaison-la-Romaine
Last two weeks of July: Festival of Music and Dance.
Aix-en-Provence
Last week of July: Festival of Music.
Beaumes-de-Venise
Last Sunday in July: local festival.
Cotignac
Late July–early August: Festival de la Falaise, theatre and music.
Gordes
Between the last weekend of July and the first weekend of August: Festival of Theatre and Music.

AUGUST

Ramatuelle
First two weeks of August: Festival of Theatre and Music.
La Ciotat
Festival of Cinema.
Châteauneuf-du-Pape
Wine Festival.
St Remy
15 August: Provençal Festival.
Seguret
Third week in August: Provençal Festival.
Apt
Last Sunday in August: Festival of St-Anne.

SEPTEMBER

Les-Saintes-Maries-de-la-Mer
1st Sunday in September: Pilgrimage.
Arles
Mid-September: Premices du Riz (the rice harvest festival).

NOVEMBER

Avignon
Mid-November: Festival of the Côtes du Rhône *primeurs* (first wines).

DECEMBER

Les Baux
Christmas Eve: La Fête du Pastrage.
Seguret
Christmas Eve: Festival of the Nativity.
Arles
Late December/early January: Salon International des Santonniers, an event which gathers together nativity scenes and *santons*.

Practical Information

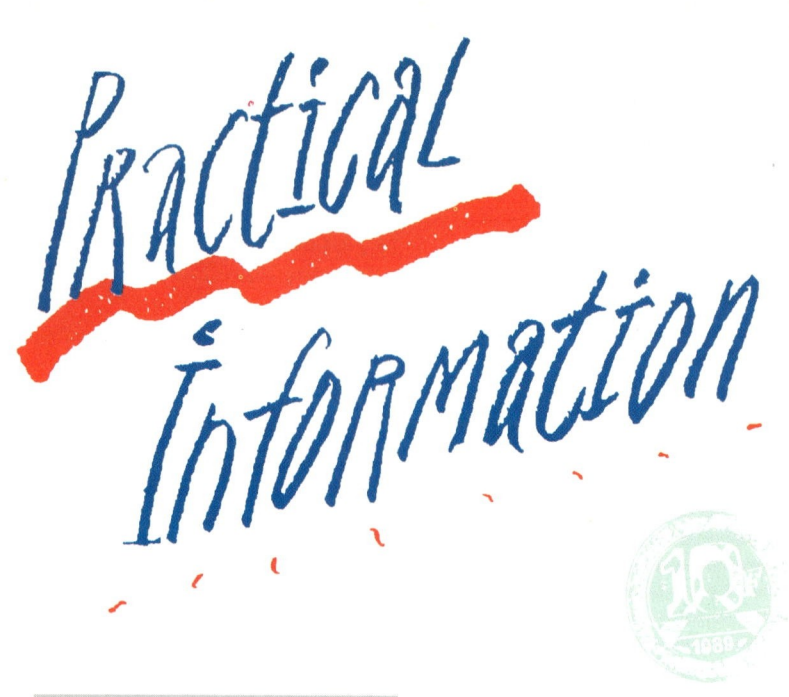

GETTING THERE

By Air
Provence has two international airports, Marseille-Provence and Nice-Côte d'Azur. Marseille-Provence, less than 20km (12 miles) from both Aix and Marseille, is certainly a more convenient destination for the area covered in this guide.

Nice airport has more direct international flights and more charter flights (particularly from London) and therefore better deals. However connections are simply made from Paris to both Marseille and Nice, with at least 20 Air France and Air Inter flights daily.

Both airports operate a regular *navette* (bus) to the main line railway stations. If you arrive very late on a charter flight you might have to wait for the first bus in the morning.

All the main car hire companies are represented at both airports. Normally they wait for the last flight; again it can happen that the shutters are down if you arrive very late.

By Rail
This is a magnificent way to travel to Provence, especially on the TGV, *train à grande vitesse*. From Paris it takes 3hrs 45 minutes to Avignon, 4hrs 40 minutes to Marseille.

Neither Aix nor Arles are on the main line, but they are both linked by local lines to Marseille and Avignon respectively.

Touring Provence by train is not an option. The Romans had a more extensive network of roads in Provence than SNCF has railway lines.

By Car
A car is essential to make the most of

Provence, and the *Conseil Regional* – the regional authority – has recognised this and devoted considerable resources to improving the secondary road system. It is now excellent.

Hiring a car in France is expensive, rarely less than £40 a day, even for a small model. There are companies, such as Euro Express in England (Tel: 0293 511125), who sell flight and car packages which reduce this cost. They might provide a good solution for an autumn weekend in Arles.

Driving to Provence from Paris and the North involves ploughing down the *autoroute du soleil*, and paying some fairly heavy tolls.

If you are determined to avoid the motorways, you could follow the *itinéraires bis* (after the *bison futé* – crafty bison – whose symbol used to advertise the roads). They were invented to help drivers avoid traffic jams through France. A map of these routes can be obtained from motorway tourist offices.

Driving

You should carry in the car at all times a full driving licence, your vehicle registration document and evidence of insurance cover. You are also required to carry a red warning triangle for breakdowns and a spare set of bulbs.

Seat belts must be worn by the driver and all passengers. Full or dipped headlights must be used at night (not side lights). If you have a right-hand drive vehicle it is important either to tint headlights yellow or apply special stickers which regulate the beam. This is both a matter of safety and courtesy.

Speed Limits

Urban areas, 60kph (37mph).
Single carriageway roads, 90kph (56mph); on wet roads 80kph/50mph.
Dual carriageway roads, 110kph (68mph); on wet roads 100kph/62mph.
Motorways, 130kph (80mph); on wet roads 110kph/68mph.

Speeding offences are subject to an on-the-spot fine of 900FF.
Drinking and driving is also heavily penalised by on-the-spot fines and confiscation of the vehicle.

TRAVEL ESSENTIALS

Visas and Passports
All persons entering France must possess a current, valid passport. Visitors from outside the EC, Andorra, Monaco, Switzerland and North America also require a visa. They can be obtained for a nominal fee from any French consulate.

When to Visit
Statistics boast 2,500–2,800 hours of sun each year. There are clear, sunny days at all times of the year. Sun and heat are virtually guaranteed in July and August. There is a marked change at the end of August, when a few spectacular thunderstorms race through the region and the mistral is more likely to blow. As a result, the light has a special brilliancy in September and October.

I have the impression that the mistral, the famous wind of Provence, is less in evidence than it was. Referred to in Provençal mythology as *le maître* (the master), it is said to blow 170 days a year in some areas of Provence. Technically the wind is born in the plain of Valence where cold air from the mountains is attracted by huge masses of warm air over the Mediterranean. It starts with particular gusto when a depression of warm air comes up from the southern Mediterranean. Bottled into a narrow corridor, the wind accelerates rapidly and is uncorked in the Bouches-du-Rhône, its effects felt all over the Vaucluse and the Var.

The months of November and December are likely to be wet, but around Christmas the weather is often clear, and you can eat outside at midday (nights, however, are cold). The temperature climbs from the end of March but the weather will be variable until the end of June – periods of very warm weather, interspersed with unsettled weather.

The itineraries in this book are geared to the summer months of July and August, when Provence is *en fête*, animated by innumerable festivals – but also particularly crowded by the coast.

Clothing
Take cool, comfortable, casual clothes in summer. Don't forget a sun hat, dark glasses and sun cream and a sweater for the evening. At other times of year dress as for any temperate climate.

Electricity
France runs on 220V, with double, round-pin sockets. A socket adaptor is required for the British 3-pin plug. A voltage transformer will be required for electrical goods that originated in countries, such as the USA, where the current alternates at 60 cycles and not the European standard of 50 cycles.

Time
France is in the Continental European time zone. It is one hour ahead of British time, 6 and 9 hours respectively ahead of the US time zones, Eastern Standard Time and Pacific Standard Time.

MONEY MATTERS

Banks
Opening hours: Tuesday–Saturday, 9am–noon, 2–4.30pm. In some towns one of the banks opens on a Monday.

Currency
The units of the currency are francs and centimes. Denominations: notes, 500FF, 200FF, 100FF, 50FF and 20FF; coins, 10FF, 5FF, 2FF, 1FF; and 50, 20, 10 and 5 centime pieces.

Credit Cards
Credit cards have a wide but by no means universal currency in Provence. The economy is still cash based. The 'market' economy is certainly lubricated by *le liquide* (cash). Many wine producers and restaurants do not accept cards. Eurocheques and traveller's cheques are useful resources.

Cash Machines
The hole in the wall has arrived in Provence. In theory PIN numbers are universally recognised. Cash machines are especially useful on Monday, when banks are closed.

Tipping
This is included in the bill in restaurants, hotels and cafés. Exceptional service can be rewarded with a tip, the *pourboire* (literally, 'for a drink'). Hairdressers, taxi drivers, porters and doormen expect a small tip.

HOLIDAYS & HOURS

Business Hours
The lunch break is still sacrosanct in Provence – in many villages noon is announced by a siren. Banks, tourist offices, museums, shops, petrol stations, post offices, almost everything, will close for two hours.

The basic working hours are 9am–noon and 2–6pm, although supermarkets and other shops staying open until 7.30 or 8pm do not re-open until 3.30pm.

The working week is generally Tuesday–Saturday; even quite big towns can be deserted on a Monday.

Public Holidays
There are 12 *jours fériés*, or public holidays.
1 January
Easter Monday
1 May
8 May (V-E Day)
Ascension Thursday
Whit Monday (the Monday following the seventh Sunday after Easter)
14 July (Bastille Day)
15 August (Assumption)
1 November (All Saints' Day)
11 November (Armistice Day 1918)
Christmas Day
26 December

Closed for lunch?

Hotel Crillon Le Brave

ACCOMMODATION

Hotels

The local Tourist Office can be very helpful if you have trouble finding accommodation. They will have lists of *gîtes*, self-catering holiday cottages, rentable for the weekend or for several weeks, *chambres d'hôtes*, the French equivalent of bed and breakfast, and camping sites – which are often superb.

The following list of recommendations is structured so that it follows the man sections of this guide. Price indications given are based on single occupancy: $=150FF or less; $$=150-300FF; $$$=300-450FF; $$$$=450-700FF; $$$$$=700FF or more. Breakfast is not included in the price.

Vaucluse

Bédoin

HOTEL RESTAURANT L'ESCAPADE
Tel: 90 65 60 21.
Has a good restaurant that is great value. Look out for the *menu du jour* at 60FF. $

HOTEL DES PINS
Tel: 90 65 60 96. $$

Bédoin has an excellent municipal camp site; Tel: 90 65 61 03. Any number of *gîtes* can be found in this area, details from the Tourist Office: Tel: 90 65 63 95.

HOTEL CRILLON LE BRAVE
Tel: 90 65 61 61.
Can there be a more beautiful hotel in Provence? Situated in a stunning location opposite Mt-Ventoux. Lovely gardens, good restaurant and superb rooms decorated in Provençal style. $$$$$

Vaison-la-Romaine

HOTEL LE BEFFROI
Tel: 90 36 04 71.
Interesting hotel in the *haute ville*; a good restaurant and 17th-century *salon* with original beamed ceiling and fireplace. $$$

HOTEL BURRHUS
Tel: 90 36 00 11.
In the busy Place Montfort. $$

Seguret

HOTEL RESTAURANT LA TABLE DU COMTAT
Tel: 90 46 91 49.
Eight bedrooms, superb restaurant, perfect setting. $$$$

La Table du Comta

Avignon

HOTEL EUROPE
12 Place Crillon.
Tel: 90 82 66 92.
Probably Avignon's best hotel. Once a coaching inn, mentioned in many early travellers' accounts. Very quiet and comfortable. *$$$$*

HOTEL DU PALAIS DES PAPES
Tel: 90 86 04 13.
Good, old-style hotel opposite the Palais des Papes. *$$*

REGINA HOTEL
6 Rue de la République.
Tel: 90 86 49 45.
Just off the Place de l'Horloge, a nicely modernised hotel. They have a few bedrooms for four people at 370 francs, which is quite a bargain for the centre of Avignon. *$$*

HOTEL MIGNON
12 Rue Joseph-Vernet.
Tel: 90 82 17 30.
Mignon means cute or sweet in French, and it is. *$*

HOTEL SAINT-GEORGE
12 Rue de l'Etoile.
Tel: 90 88 54 34.
Outside the ramparts on the road to Marseille. Clean, friendly and good value. *$*

Collias

HOSTELLERIE LE CASTELLAS
Tel: 66 22 88 88.
A converted 17th-century governor's mansion, a delight to stay here. *$$$*

Arles

GRAND HOTEL NORD-PINUS
Place du Forum.
Tel: 90 93 44 44.
If I could choose to stay anywhere in Arles it would be here. A luxury hotel redolent with the history and culture of Arles, particularly when its superb bar 'La Corrida' is packed with matadors and their flamboyant retinues. *$$$$*

HOTEL DU FORUM
Place du Forum.
Tel: 90 93 48 95.
Lacks the style of the Nord-Pinus but a comfortable hotel with the great advantage of a swimming pool in a secluded courtyard. *$$$*

Hotel du Forum

HOTEL D'ARLATEN
26 Rue du Sauvage.
Tel: 90 93 56 66.
The beautifully restored home of the Counts of Arlaten, just off Place du Forum. *$$$*

HOTEL LE CLOITRE
16 Rue du Cloître.
Tel: 90 96 29 50.
Quiet, Provençal style hotel in a narrow street behind the Cloisters. *$$*

HOTEL DE LA MUETTE
15 Rue des Suisses.
Tel: 90 96 15 39. $$

HOTEL CALENDAL
22 Place Pomme.
Tel: 90 96 11 89.
Good rooms and a shady garden behind the Arena. $$

HOTEL DIDEROT
9 Rue de la Bastille.
Tel: 90 96 10 30. $

St Remy

HOTEL DES ANTIQUES
15 Avenue Pasteur.
Tel: 90 92 03 02.
Fin de siècle charm, lovely garden – you could call it a park – and pool. $$$

HOTEL DE PROVENCE
36 Boulevard Victor Hugo.
Tel: 90 92 06 27. $

Aix-en-Provence

LE PIGONNET
5 Avenue du Pigonnet.
Tel: 42 59 02 90.
Expensive old country house hotel, in a tree-filled park in the middle of Aix. $$$$$

LE MANOIR
8 Rue d'Entrecasteaux.
Tel: 42 26 27 20.
Comfortable old-style hotel, breakfast in the 14th-century cloister. $$

HOTEL DES AUGUSTINS
3 Rue de la Masse.
Tel: 42 27 28 59.
Another impressive hotel in an old religious house. On the corner of the Cours and Rue de la Masse. Two of the rooms have private terraces. $$$$

HOTEL DES QUATRE DAUPHINS
54 Rue Roux Alphéran.
Tel: 42 38 16 39.
In the Mazarin quarter, near the fountain of the same name. $$

HOTEL SPLENDID
69 Cours Mirabeau.
Tel: 42 38 19 53.
You won't miss a beat here. Good value but not for those who like to sleep early. $

Along the Coast

Cassis

LE LIATAUD
Place Clemenceau.
Tel: 42 01 75 37.
Breakfast room overlooks the port; restaurant has a good reputation. $$

Cassis has a good camping site 10-minutes' walk from the sea: Les Cigales, route de Marseille; Tel: 42 01 07 34.

Bormes-les-Mimosas

LE GRAND HOTEL
167 Route de Baguier.
Tel: 94 71 23 72.
Old-style hotel in a garden of palms overlooking the village. $$

LE LAURENCE
8 Rue de l'Arène.
Tel: 42 01 88 78.
Near the port, with peaceful terrace. $$

Hyères-Plage
Hotel la Méditerranée
Avenue de la Méditerranée.
Tel: 94 58 03 89.
A good place to stay if you are visiting Porquerolles. *$$*

Gassin
Hotel Restaurant Bello Visto
Place des Barrys.
Tel: 94 56 17 30.
Also a good restaurant, one of a number on the *place* with terraces looking towards the bay of Pampelonne. *$$*

St-Tropez
Recommending hotels in St-Tropez is easy; finding a room if you have not booked well in advance is difficult, probably impossible in the summer.

Hotel de la Ponche
Place du Revelin.
Tel: 94 97 02 53.
Closed from 15 October–1 April. Hotel formed from a number of old fishermen's cottages. Exquisitely furnished. *$$$$$*

La Méditerranée
21 Boulevard Louis Blanc.
Tel: 94 97 00 44.
Open from Easter to December. *$$$$*

Lou Cagnard
18 Avenue P Roussel.
Tel: 94 97 04 24.
Open all year. More peaceful position towards the rear of the town, behind the Place des Lices. *$$*

The Var

Entrecasteaux
Chateau d'Entrecasteaux
Tel: 94 04 43 95.
The ultimate bed and breakfast establishment. *$$$$$*

Salernes
Hotel Allegre
20 Rue J J Rousseau.
Tel: 94 70 60 30.
Everything about this hotel is *correct* and unchanging. The restaurant has a good reputation locally. *$$*

Cotignac
Hostellerie Lou Calen
1 Cours Gambetta.
Tel: 94 04 60 40.
One of the best hotels in the area, with a shady garden and a large swimming pool. Restaurant has a good reputation. *$$$*

Hotel Restaurant du Cours
Tel: 94 04 66 34.
A good budget hotel with *pension complet* from 210FF. The restaurant has a 55FF menu including wine. *$*

Aups
Auberge de la Tour
Rue Abbé Aloisi.
Tel: 94 70 00 30.
The smartest spot in the town. Good pizzas. *$$*

Grand Hotel
Place Gendarme-Duchatel.
Tel: 94 70 00 89.
Friendly, *correct* hotel. The place for the *menu du jour* – 60FF including wine. *$$*

Le Provençal
Place Bidouret.
Tel: 94 70 00 24.
Small, rustic hotel. *$$*

Tourtour
Bastide de Tourtour
Tel: 94 70 57 30.
Menus range from 280FF to 390FF. Luxury. *$$$$$*

La Petite Auberge
1km (½ mile) south of the village on the D77.
Tel: 94 70 57 16.
Imagine having the view that you see from the orientation point from your bedroom. Add a swimming pool and a good restaurant and you have something special. $$$

Villecroze-les-Grottes
Grand Hotel
Tel: 94 70 78 82.
Good location on the *cours*, not exactly grand but nicely modernised. $

The Luberon

Apt
Auberge du Luberon
17 Quai Léon-Sagy.
Tel: 90 74 12 50.
The best hotel in Apt, across the river from the Place de la Bouquerie. Good restaurant. $$$

Hotel le Ventoux
67 Avenue Victor-Hugo.
Tel: 90 74 07 58.
Opposite the station on the busy road to Avignon. $$

Hotel le Palais
Place Gabriel Péri.
Tel: 90 04 89 32.
Good cheap rooms in the middle of town. $

Hotel l'Aptois
Cours Lauze de Perret.
Tel: 90 74 02 02. $$

Roussillon
Hotel 'Résidence des Ocres'
Route de Gordes.
Tel: 90 05 60 50.
In the heart of the village, air-conditioned rooms. $$

Gordes
Les Bories
On the D177 to Sénanque.
Tel: 90 72 00 51.
This began life as a rustic hostel in a few *bories*. It is still talked of in those terms but, make no mistake, this is now a luxury hotel. Fixed price lunch. $$$$

La Mayanelle
6 Rue Combe.
Tel: 90 72 00 28.
Down from the main square, fine views. $$

Le Provençal
Place du Château.
Tel: 90 72 01 07. $$

Auberge de Carcarille
2km east of Gordes on the D2.
Tel: 90 72 02 63.
In the countryside; has a swimming pool. Restaurant considered to be good for the prices. $$

Bonnieux
Hotel César
Place de la Liberté.
Tel: 90 75 80 18.
Dining room looks out over the valley to Lacoste. $$

NIGHTLIFE

Come meet me in some dead café –
A puff of cognac or a sip of smoke.
(from *Avignon* by Lawrence Durrell)

Nightlife in Provence is sitting in the Place du Forum in Arles listening to a saxophone and bass improvise around the chords of *Round Midnight;* it is ordering just one last bottle of rosé with the patron yawning; it is the village ball and *fête*. It might be drinking a coffee or promenading on the Cours Mirabeau, or

Nightlife coming to the Place du Forum, Arles

listening to the string quartet on the terrace of the château in Entrecasteaux. It is occasionally an open-air film, the festival of theatre in Avignon, classical music in Aix or jazz in Hyères. It can be the nightclub, but that is really the preserve of the coast and above all St-Tropez, and it disappears completely in winter.

The best guides to what is on are the local papers and a listings magazine, published on Wednesday, called *La Semaine des Spectacles*.

HEALTH & EMERGENCIES

The number for the emergency services is 15.

France has one of the best national health services in the world. In 1984 health spending was 9.7 percent of GDP; Britain's figure was 4.8 percent. A structural difference is that in France the patient pays many of the costs up front and 75–80 percent are reimbursed. For example, doctors charge 100FF for each consultation.

The advantage for the visitor is that there is little bureaucracy; doctors and hospitals will treat everyone without worrying about whether a patient is a member of their scheme or health authority.

Citizens of the EC are entitled to health care in France on the same terms as the French; that is, payment and reimbursement by their own government. British citizens will find this process is smoother if the doctor or hospital giving treatment fills out form E111 (obtainable in Britain before you leave).

Refunds extend to any medicines prescribed by the doctor. Be warned: doctors in France prescribe very freely and the pharmacies, though excellent, are expensive. They are one of the last cartels, enjoying a monopoly of the sale of all medicines, even aspirins. One point in their favour is that a pharmacist has considerable powers to prescribe medicine. For minor problems they should be consulted before a doctor.

As in any country it is an advantage to have your own private medical insurance.

Police and Crime
The number for an emergency is 17.

Petty theft is inevitably a problem in the bigger towns and on the coast, less so in rural areas. Tape decks and luggage in cars are the usual targets. Thefts should be reported to the local *gendarmerie*, who will reluctantly

Guardians of the law in Aix

issue the papers necessary for an insurance claim – don't go at lunch time.

Fires
The number for an emergency is 18.

Forest fires are a perennial problem in Provence, and fire fighting equipment is in place in every *commune*. Devastation every year is severe; the heavily forested department of the Var suffers most.

Cooking on an open fire in the forest and *camping sauvage* (outside designated sites) are both forbidden in Provence, and infringements are heavily penalised. You should be very careful with cigarette ends, etc.

POST & COMMUNICATIONS

Post
Post offices are generally open 9am –noon and 2–5pm, Monday–Friday and 9am–noon on Saturday. Stamps, *des timbres*, are also sold from *tabacs*, which can be found in many bars.

Telephone
Twenty years ago a popular saying went, 'Half the nation is waiting for a phone to be installed and the other half for a dialling tone.' Today France has one of the best telecommunications systems in Europe.

It is wise to equip yourself with a phone card because rapid modernisation has made the coin box obsolete in many areas, though you can usually find one in the local bar.

To call other countries, first dial the international access code **19**: **Australia** (61); **Germany** (49); **Italy** (39); **Netherlands** (31); **Spain** (34); UK (44); US and **Canada** (1). If using a US credit phone card, call the company's access number below: AT&T, Tel: 11-0010; MCI, Tel: 078 11-0012; Sprint, Tel: 078 11-0014.

Media
France does not have a national press as in Britain, or share the same obsession with newspapers. Regional and provincial papers account for over two-thirds of the daily sale, a pattern similar to the US. Newspapers such as *Le Provençal* and *Var Matin* have only a few pages of hard news but are excellent sources of local information of all kinds.

INFORMATION & MAPS

The itineraries in this guide have been put together with the assumption that anyone following them will also have a good map. I recommend either Michelin map no. 245, in the series 1cm: 2km (coloured yellow), or map number 115 in the *Institut Géographique National* red series, 1cm: 2½km.

Local tourist offices are good sources for town plans and local maps, and for information regarding opening hours of museums and other local attractions, as well as restaurants.

In the Vaucluse such offices are very strong on publicising outdoor activities and supply maps designed for walkers and cyclists.

LANGUAGE

The curiosity of the French language in Provence is the accent. Many words finish with a kind of clanging sound. Other European languages are increasingly well known.

The most important thing to remember is that the *rapports sociale* are more formal than in many countries, witness the shaking of hands and the ritual of the *bise* (kiss).

The following are used all the time and are essential:

Good morning/hello	*Bonjour*
Good evening	*Bonsoir*
How are you?	*Comment allez-vous?*
I'm well	*Très bien, merci*
Goodbye	*Au revoir*
Please	*S'il vous plaît*
Yes please	*S'il vous plaît*
Thank you	*Merci*
You are welcome	*Je vous en prie*
Enjoy your meal	*Bon appetit*
See you later	*A tout à l'heure*

USEFUL ADDRESSES

Tourist Offices

Aix-en-Provence: Place de Général de Gaulle, 13100 Aix-en-Provence.
Apt: Place Bouquerie, 84400 Apt.
Arles: Esplanade Charles de Gaulle, 13200 Arles.
Avignon: 41 Cours Jean Jaurès, 84000 Avignon.
Aups: Place Mairie, 83630 Aups.
Bédoin: 84410 Bédoin.
Cassis: Place P Baragnon, 13260 Cassis.
Salernes: Rue Victor Hugo, 83690 Salernes.
St Tropez: Gare Routière, 83990 St-Tropez.
Vaison-la-Romaine: Place du Chanoine Sautel, 84110 Vaison.
London: French Tourist Office, 178 Piccadilly, London W1V 9DB. Tel: 071 491 7622.
New York: French Tourist Office, 610 Fifth Avenue, # 222, New York, NY 10020-2452. Tel: 212 757 1125.

FURTHER READING

Travels Through France and Italy by Tobias Smollett, The World's Classics, Oxford University Press, 1990.
Hills and the Sea by Hilaire Belloc, Methuen & Co, 1906.
Letters from My Windmill by Alphonse Daudet, Penguin, 1982.
Collected Stories by Colette, Penguin, 1985.
Petrarch and his World by Morris Bishop, Chatto & Windus, 1964.
The Waning of the Middle Ages by J Huizinga, Penguin, 1990 (classic study, good on the Courts of Love).
Provence by Ford Madox Ford, Allen & Unwin, 1938.
Insight Guide: Provence, APA Publications, 1992.
Insight Guide: Côte D'Azur, APA Publications, 1992.
Insight Pocket Guide: Côte D'Azur, APA Publications, 1993.
The Wines of the Rhône Valley and Provence by Robert Parker, Dorling Kindersley, 1987.

Index

A

'aïoli' 34, 71, 73
Aix-en-Provence 13, 14, 42–6
Apt 60–1
arena (amphithéâtre) 36, 40
Arles 36–40
Aups 57–8
Avignon 30–3

B

Bandol 50
Bardot, Brigitte 17, 52
baroque 45
beaches 53–4
Beaumes-de-Venise 27
Belloc, Hilaire 37–8
Bonnieux 63–4
'bories' (stone huts) 62
'bouillabaisse' 47
'Bravade' 16
bullfights 36

C

'calanques' 49–50
'calissons' 45
Camargue 41
Cassis 49–50
Cathédrale d'Images 39
ceramics, ceramic tiles 56, 58
Cézanne, Paul 17, 44–6
Chateau of Entrecasteaux 56–7
Chateauneuf-du-Pape 33–4
Chateaux la Canorgue 64
Christianity 14–5
Cistercians 15, 63
Colette 17, 52
Côte d'Azur 48
Cotignac 57
Cours Julien 47
Cours Mirabeau 43–5
courtly love tradition 40

D, E

Daudet, Alphonse 34
Dentelles de Montmirail 23, 27
Dickens, Charles 45
Doms garden 33
Etang de Vaccarès (nature reserve) 41
Evelyn, John 31

F

'faïence' 67, 68
Festival d'Avignon 31–2
'Felibrige' 18
Festival of Music (Aix) 42
'fêtes' 15–6
'fête et pélerinage' 16
'fêtes' of the Nativity 15, 25
fish 49, 50
folk culture 36–7
Ford, Madox Ford 12
fountains 43, 44
fruit 13, 60

G, I, K

Gigondas 26–7
glacé fruits(speciality) 61
Gordes 62–3
Grand Canyon du Verdon 59
Greeks 12–3
Ile de Porquerolles 51
Iles d'Hyères 51
kayaks 35

L

L'Ile-sur-la-Sorgue 35
Lac de Ste-Croix 59
'langue d'oc' (Provençal language) 18
lavender, lavender honey 29, 63
Le Moulin de Maître Cornille 38
Les Alpilles 39
Les Baux 39–40
Les-Saintes-Maries-de-la-Mer 16, 41
Louis II of Anjou 42
Luberon, the 60–4

M

Malaucène 23, 29
markets 35, 56, 61, 66–9
Marseille 47
Mausanne 38
McGarvie-Munn, Ian 56
Mirabeau, Count of 43
mistral 28, 41
Mistral, Frédéric 37
Mont St-Victoire 45–6
mosquitoes 41
Mt-Ventoux 23, 28
Musée de la Boulangerie 63–4
Musée Granet 44
Muséon Arlaten 37

N, O

Nord-Pinus Hotel 14, 38
nougat 29
olive oil, olive trees 38–9
olives 13

P

papacy, papal court 15,18, 31, 34
Palais des Papes 32–3
Paradu 38
perched villages 63
Picasso, Pablo 46
Place de l'Horloge 32–3
Place du Forum 38, 40
Pont du Gard (aqueduct) 34–5
Pont Julien 60, 64
Pont St-Bénézet (the bridge of Avignon) 33

Q, R

Quartier de Puymin 24
Quartier Mazarin 44
Religious Wars 15
Renaissance 42, 44, 62
René, Count of Provence 42
Romanesque 15
Romans 13–4, 42
Roussillon 61–2

S

sailboarding 51
Saintes-Maries-de-la-Mer (*see* Les-Saintes-Maries-de-la-Mer)
Salernes 55–6
'santons' 15, 25, 68
Sault 29
Seguret 25
Sénanque abbey 63
Signac, Paul 17, 52
Smollett, Tobias 16
Souleiado 67–8
St-Firmin church 63
St-Tropez 16, 17, 52–4
St-Trophime church 37–8

T, U

Théâtre Antique (Arles) 40
thermal springs 14, 42
Tour de France 28
troubadours 40
university (Aix) 42
Uzès 35

V, W

Vaison-la-Romaine 23–4
Van Gogh, Vincent 17, 38
Var, the 55–9
Villecroze-les-Grottes 58
vineyards 12–3, 33, 37
wine 13, 25–7, 34, 50–1, 54, 55, 57, 63–4, 68

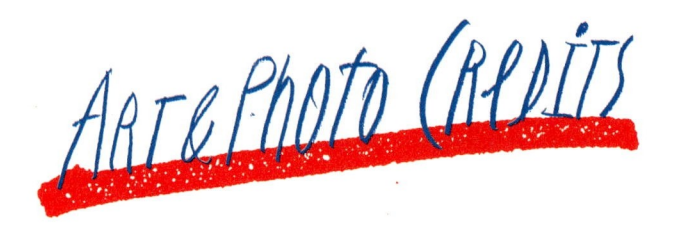

Art & Photo Credits

Photography	Gil Galvin and George Taylor *and*
Pages 10/11, 36B, 43, 79	Catherine Karnow
Production Editor	Erich Meyer
Cover Design	Klaus Geisler
Cartography	Berndtson & Berndtson

EXISTING & FORTHCOMING TITLES:

Aegean Islands	Ireland	Phuket
Algarve	Istanbul	Prague
Alsace	**J**akarta	Provence
Athens	**K**athmandu	**R**hodes
Bali	*Bikes & Hikes*	Rome
Bali Bird Walks	Kenya	**S**abah
Bangkok	Kuala Lumpur	San Francisco
Barcelona	**L**isbon	Sardinia
Bavaria	Loire Valley	Scotland
Berlin	London	Seville/Grenada
Bhutan	**M**acau	Seychelles
Boston	Madrid	Sikkim
Brittany	Malacca	Singapore
Brussels	Mallorca	South California
Budapest &	Malta	Southeast England
Surroundings	Marbella/	Sri Lanka
Canton	*Costa del Sol*	St Petersburg
Chiang Mai	Miami	Sydney
Costa Blanca	Milan	**T**enerife
Costa Brava	Morocco	Thailand
Cote d'Azur	Moscow	Tibet
Crete	Munich	Turkish Coast
Denmark	**N**epal	Tuscany
Florence	New Delhi	**V**enice
Florida	New York City	Vienna
Gran Canaria	North California	**Y**ogyakarta
Hawaii	**O**slo/Bergen	Yugoslavia's
Hong Kong	**P**aris	*Adriatic Coast*
Ibiza	Penang	

• •

United States: **Houghton Mifflin Company, Boston MA 02108**
Tel: (800) 2253362 Fax: (800) 4589501

Canada: **Thomas Allen & Son, 390 Steelcase Road East**
Markham, Ontario L3R 1G2
Tel: (416) 4759126 Fax: (416) 4756747

Great Britain: **GeoCenter UK, Hampshire RG22 4BJ**
Tel: (256) 817987 Fax: (256) 817988

Worldwide: **Höfer Communications Singapore 2262**
Tel: (65) 8612755 Fax: (65) 8616438

❝ I was first drawn to the Insight Guides by the excellent "Nepal" volume. I can think of no book which so effectively captures the essence of a country. Out of these pages leaped the Nepal I know – the captivating charm of a people and their culture. I've since discovered and enjoyed the entire Insight Guide Series. Each volume deals with a country or city in the same sensitive depth, which is nowhere more evident than in the superb photography. ❞

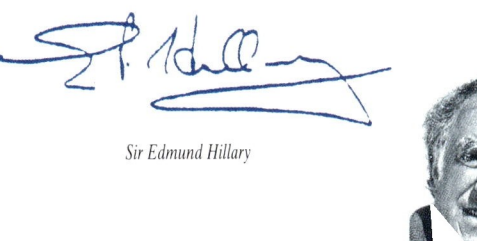

Sir Edmund Hillary

COLORSET NUMBERS

- 160 **A**laska
- 155 Alsace
- 150 Amazon Wildlife
- 116 America, South
- 173 American Southwest
- 158A Amsterdam
- 260 Argentina
- 287 Asia, East
- 207 Asia, South
- 262 Asia, South East
- 194 Asian Wildlife, Southeast
- 167A Athens
- 272 Australia
- 263 Austria
- 188 **B**ahamas
- 206 Bali Baru
- 107 Baltic States
- 246A Bangkok
- 292 Barbados
- 219B Barcelona
- 187 Bay of Naples
- 234 Beijing
- 109 Belgium
- 135A Berlin
- 217 Bermuda
- 100A Boston
- 127 Brazil
- 178 Brittany
- 109A Brussels
- 144A Budapest
- 260A Buenos Aires
- 213 Burgundy
- 268A **C**airo
- 247B Calcutta
- 275 California
- 180 California, Northern
- 161 California, Southern
- 237 Canada
- 162 Caribbean The Lesser Antilles
- 122 Catalonia (Costa Brava)
- 141 Channel Islands
- 184C Chicago
- 151 Chile
- 234 China
- 135E Cologne
- 119 Continental Europe
- 189 Corsica
- 281 Costa Rica
- 291 Cote d'Azur
- 165 Crete
- 184 Crossing America
- 226 Cyprus
- 114 Czechoslovakia
- 247A **D**elhi, Jaipur, Agra
- 238 Denmark
- 135B Dresden
- 142B Dublin
- 135F Düsseldorf
- 204 **E**ast African Wildlife
- 149 Eastern Europe,
- 118 Ecuador
- 148A Edinburgh
- 268 Egypt
- 123 **F**inland
- 209B Florence
- 243 Florida
- 154 France
- 135C Frankfurt
- 208 **G**ambia & Senegal
- 135 Germany
- 148B Glasgow
- 279 Gran Canaria
- 169 Great Barrier Reef
- 124 Great Britain
- 167 Greece
- 166 Greek Islands
- 135G **H**amburg
- 240 Hawaii
- 193 Himalaya, Western
- 196 Hong Kong
- 144 Hungary
- 256 **I**celand
- 247 India
- 212 India, South
- 128 Indian Wildlife
- 143 Indonesia
- 142 Ireland
- 252 Israel
- 236A Istanbul
- 209 Italy
- 213 **J**amaica
- 278 Japan
- 266 Java
- 252A Jerusalem-Tel Aviv
- 203A **K**athmandu
- 270 Kenya
- 300 Korea
- 202A **L**isbon
- 258 Loire Valley
- 124A London
- 275A Los Angeles
- 201 **M**adeira
- 219A Madrid
- 145 Malaysia
- 157 Mallorca & Ibiza
- 117 Malta
- 272B Melbourne
- 285 Mexico
- 285A Mexico City
- 243 Miami
- 237B Montreal
- 235 Morocco
- 101A Moscow
- 135D Munich
- 211 Myanmar (Burma)
- 259 **N**amibia
- 269 Native America
- 203 Nepal
- 158 Netherlands
- 100 **N**ew England
- 184E New Orleans
- 184F New York City
- 133 New York State
- 293 New Zealand
- 265 Nile, The
- 120 Norway
- 124B **O**xford
- 147 **P**acific Northwest
- 205 Pakistan
- 154A Paris
- 249 Peru
- 184B Philadelphia
- 222 Philippines
- 115 Poland
- 202 Portugal
- 114A Prague
- 153 Provence
- 156 Puerto Rico
- 250 **R**ajasthan
- 177 Rhine
- 127A Rio de Janeiro
- 172 Rockies
- 209A Rome
- 101 Russia
- 275B **S**an Francisco
- 130 Sardinia
- 148 Scotland
- 184D Seattle
- 261 Sicily
- 159 Singapore
- 257 South Africa
- 264 South Tyrol
- 219 Spain
- 220 Spain, Southern
- 105 Sri Lanka
- 101B St Petersburg
- 170 Sweden
- 232 Switzerland
- 272 Sydney
- 175 **T**aiwan
- 112 Tenerife
- 186 Texas
- 246 Thailand
- 278A Tokyo
- 139 Trinidad & Tobago
- 113 Tunisia
- 236 Turkey
- 171 Turkish Coast
- 210 Tuscany
- 174 Umbria
- 237A **V**ancouver
- 198 Venezuela
- 209C Venice
- 263A Vienna
- 255 Vietnam
- 267 **W**ales
- 184C Washington DC
- 183 Waterways of Europe
- 215 **Y**emen

You'll find the colorset number on the spine of each Insight Guide.